ENDORSEMENTS

"Here is the companion we need for our study of the book of Hebrews. The clear exposition of Scripture, real stories, and penetrating insights from the original language enrich our personal relationship with Christ. Jeremy Vance is a godly pastor-teacher and this book needs to be one of our resources for a practical and a homiletical study of the book of Hebrews."

> — Dr. Richard Gentry Thompson
> Great Lakes District Superintendent
> Evangelical Free Church of America

I have taken the classes, read the commentaries, and have preached on Hebrews, but this is indeed a fresh, insightful, and thought provoking journey through Hebrews. In most commentaries you read the passage and the author tries to explain it. But here the author often presents real life issues, the answers for which are found in the passages. Pastor Vance does not shy away from the "warning passages"; actually he dives in with insight and thoughtful persuasion. Is it a commentary, yes, and where needed a scholarly work. Is it a devotional, yes, with helpful anecdotes from his own life. But it is more; it is purposefully designed to deepen your journey as a "companion with Christ" (taken from the Greek term *metochos*, which appears five times in Hebrews). AND, your audience will appreciate the fact that you consulted this work when you again prepare to preach or teach through this marvelous portion of scripture.

> — Gaylen J. Nagel
> District Superintendent
> Forest Lakes District
> Evangelical Free Church of America

"Companions With Christ brings the weighty truths of Hebrews to the reader in a clear and understandable way. In addition, the accompanying study guide is an invaluable discipleship tool that can be used in a variety of contexts. The Body of Christ will benefit from this very practical and needed resource."

— Don Den Hartog
Pastor of Biblical Education
Fellowship Bible Church
Winchester, Virginia

If you are looking for a commentary on Hebrews that is for everybody, then go no further. Jeremy Vance displays his pastor's heart in this work on Hebrews through his use of the warning passages to encourage believers to persevere in their faith, not to hold the axe of hell over their heads if they don't. The warnings are taken to be loss of rewards in the next life as well as purpose and meaning in this life. One of the strengths of this work is the generous use of spot-on illustrations to clarify the teaching. This book will be a motivator for the devotional reader, the Sunday School teacher, or anyone trying to get a better handle on the Book of Hebrews.

— David R. Anderson, Ph.D.
President, Grace School of Theology

Companions with CHRIST

How to Walk with Jesus— A Practical Guide through the Book of Hebrews

JEREMY VANCE

I want to dedicate this book first to my parents who raised me to know Jesus and who read every chapter of this book, giving me valuable insight. Mom and Dad, you are a gift from the Lord.

I dedicate this book to Faith Church where I am serving as a pastor. It is a blessing to work with believers who are committed to God, His Word, and guiding people in the truth. To my Faith Church family, thank you for serving Jesus with me.

And most of all I want to dedicate this book to my wife, Jill. Jesus gave me a woman who loves Him first and me second. Jill, I am a blessed man to have you as my soul mate to walk with Christ together.

Cover inspired by original artwork by Allison Vance.

CONTENTS

Part III
JESUS, OUR HIGH PRIEST
Hebrews 7:1–10:25

Part IV
LIVING IN THE LIGHT OF ETERNITY
Hebrews 10:26–13:25

FOREWORD

Companions With Christ is a word of education, exhortation and encouragement from a pastor to his people. Jeremy Vance is a pastor who writes to people and whose passion in this work is to help them understand the book of Hebrews.

I first came to know Jeremy as his professor and mentor and have become his friend. He is a valued colleague in the ministry of the Lord Jesus Christ. Jeremy is a faithful pastor who labors in the word of God and who takes the advice of Ezra 7:10 to heart in that we are to *study* the word, *live* the word, and then *teach* the word to others.

The Book of Hebrews is one of the most difficult and challenging in the New Testament, given its length and its detailed use and integration of the Old Testament. It also provides a nuanced understanding of many theological concepts that are often misunderstood. This book provides a clear and smooth journey as it not only explains the rich theology of Hebrews but also provides a clear exposition of the text utilizing a sermonic style that allows for principles of penetrating personal application.

It is a skill and a sign of wisdom to be able to communicate that which is complex and make it clear. Good exposition needs to be biblically accurate and culturally relevant. This book accomplishes both objectives.

Fred Chay, PhD
Associate Professor of Theology and
Director of Doctoral Studies, Phoenix Seminary
President of Grace Line

INTRODUCTION

There once was a fighter who rose to fame for his stellar record. He had an interesting practice before every bout: before the bell rang, he would kneel in his corner and make the sign of the cross. He won one fight, and then another and another, going undefeated fight after fight. Every time, right before the bell rang, he would kneel in his corner and make the sign of the cross. Finally a reporter asked him, "Do you think making the sign of the cross helps you?" He said, "Yes sir, I do, but it also helps if you know what you're doing—if you can fight." Of course it would be too easy if being a good fighter meant all you had to do was make the sign of the cross before you fought.

As Christians, we are called to live stellar lives for Jesus's sake. And in our minds we often think what that means is doing things like praying, or reading our Bibles, or going to church. Maybe, for some of us, we even think making the sign of the cross helps. If a news reporter were to ask us if those practices help us, we would probably answer, "Yes sir, I do." But do we know what we're doing? Can we fight the good fight (2 Timothy 4:7)? We might do the things we think are expected of us when we follow Christ, but do we really know how to live the Christian life, how to walk with Jesus?

This book is about the book of Hebrews. It is not just a description of the book; it is about our spiritual formation. I felt compelled to write it because I am convinced the book of Hebrews is the most in-depth explanation in the entire Bible of what our walk with Christ is all about today. Hebrews tells us in detail how we can even have this walk with Jesus, and it explains thoroughly how our walk with Christ impacts our eternity. It has been my prayer as I have written these pages that we will learn and grow in our ability to stay in stride with Jesus, to really understand how we can be companions with Him for His mission.

Here are some opening thoughts just to set the stage:

Authorship: The author and the first recipients of the letter (or epistle) are unknown. I am inclined, for reasons I will share as we go along, to think this may very well be a sermon manuscript.

Date: Because there is no mention of the destruction of the temple in Jerusalem (AD 70) and still a reference to the sacrificial system (Hebrews 9–10), the date of the book was probably before AD 70. Yet the date is sometime after AD 49 (probably closer to AD 60) and not later than AD 90 because Timothy is still alive and active in ministry (Hebrews 13:23).

> In considering the background of Hebrews, it is reasonable to begin with the question of its date. This can be fixed within fairly good limits. The epistle can hardly be later than about AD 95 since it was known to Clement of Rome and quoted by him in 1 Clement. In addition it can scarcely be dated after AD 70, since there is no reference to the destruction of the Jewish temple in Jerusalem. Had this event already occurred, it would have given the author a definitive argument for the cessation of the Old Testament sacrificial system. Instead he seems to regard this system as still in operation (cf. 8:4, 13; 9:6–9; 10:1–3).[1]
>
> There is no need to regard 2:3 as a reference to second-generation Christians, and the epistle was obviously written during the lifetime of Timothy, whom the author knew (13:23). If the author is not Paul (and on the whole it seems likely he is not…), then 13:23 may suggest he had already died. Otherwise, Timothy might have been expected to join Paul on his release from prison. On balance, a date somewhere around AD 68 or 69 seems most likely.[2]

---

[1] The abbreviation "cf." (confer) means "compare."

[2] Walvoord and Zuck, *Bible Knowledge*, 2:777.

Outline: The book of Hebrews has been broken down in several different ways by different scholars. It appears to me there are four main parts or sections:

- The Greatness of Glory (Hebrews 1:1–5:10)
- Maturing (Hebrews 5:11–6:20)
- Jesus, Our High Priest (Hebrews 7:1–10:25)
- Living in the Light of Eternity (Hebrews 10:26–13:25)

Theme: The book of Hebrews emphasizes the importance for Christians to live as companions with Christ with a view to their future service in the kingdom to come, where the Lord will reign as the King of kings. Walking with Christ today in alignment with His Word will result in rewards in the coming kingdom rule of Jesus Christ.

Bible Version: The Bible version I use primarily is the New American Standard Bible (updated in 1995). Almost all of the English versions of the Bible are reliable, and I think the New American Standard Bible (NASB) is one of the best. It reads at about an eighth-grade level (relatively high among Bible translations); therefore, if you find any words or phrases a bit tricky, hopefully my commentary will help you understand them.

PART I
THE GREATNESS OF GLORY

Hebrews 1:1–5:10

CHAPTER ONE

WHO IS THIS JESUS?

Hebrews 1:1–14

Businesspeople call each other "team members"; the Walt Disney Company calls their employees "cast members"; soldiers call each other "comrades-in-arms" (unless, of course, you're in the navy on a ship, in which case you are a "shipmate"). What I am referring to are those who work together for a common goal, who walk in step with one another, who partner in carrying out the mission. Right off the bat, in the first words of the book of Hebrews, it is clear that God sees us as His partners; He has brought us onto His team. I know this because He communicates with us. And right now that communication and partnership are kept strong through our relationship with His Son, Jesus. Look at how Hebrews starts out:

> God, after He spoke long ago to the fathers in the prophets in many portions and in many ways, in these last days has spoken to us in His Son … (Hebrews 1:1–2a)

If our avenue for communicating with God in order to be His companions is through His Son, Jesus, it would only seem logical we would want to know who Jesus is. The author of Hebrews dedicates the first chapter to giving us five descriptions of Jesus.

He lays out the five descriptions in verses 2–3 and uses the rest of the chapter to elaborate on them.[3]

The first description of Jesus says He is an "heir." This means He inherits something; He is given ownership; He either possesses something now or will possess something in the future that He hasn't always possessed.

> in these last days has spoken to us in His Son, *whom He appointed heir of all things*, through whom also He made the world. (Hebrews 1:2)

We will find out in the pages to come that we have to be really careful with what we read. Even reading the fact that He is "appointed heir of all things" can be a bit confusing: Doesn't Jesus already own it all? Hasn't He always been the heir of all things? The author of Hebrews, under the inspiration of the Holy Spirit, lays out three things Jesus becomes the heir of by using the Old Testament to support what He inherits. First, Jesus inherits the title "Son."

> And He is the radiance of His glory and the exact representation of His nature, and upholds all things by the word of His power. When He had made purification of sins, He sat down at the right hand of the Majesty on high, having become as much better than the angels, *as He has inherited a more excellent name than they.* For to which of the angels did He ever say, "You are My Son, today I have begotten You"? And again, "I will be a Father to Him and He shall be a Son to Me"? (Hebrews 1:3–5)

The first quoted Old Testament passage is Psalm 2:7, and the second is 2 Samuel 7:14. Both references speak of the future reign of Jesus on the earth. Once Jesus ascended into heaven, God the Father gave Him the title "Son." On the one hand, Jesus always was the eternal Son of God, yet on the other hand, in line with the Old Testament quotes (especially 2 Samuel 7:14, a promise made to David approximately a thousand years earlier), Jesus would have fulfilled all that was required in order to be the Son and the King as a physical descendant of royalty—the royalty of King David. He

---

[3] We will first show those descriptions as they are laid out in verses 2–3 and then point to the verses that further explain them.

4

had to go through all He did on earth in order to be the fulfiller of the promise or covenant to David. God the Father, therefore, crowned Him Son and King.

As king and heir of all things, Jesus inherited the reign over the earth.

> And when He again brings the firstborn into the world, He says, "And let all the angels of God worship Him." And of the angels He says, "Who makes His angels winds, and His ministers a flame of fire." But of the Son He says, "Your throne, O God, is forever and ever, and the righteous scepter is the scepter of His kingdom." (Hebrews 1:6–8)

When Jesus ("the firstborn," verse 6)[4] comes again into the world and reigns on His earthly throne, the angels will worship Him as they do now in heaven.

Hebrews 1:7 is a bit challenging to understand, so let me explain it. When angels are mentioned in the Bible, it is not unheard of that fire or wind accompany their actions or describe their appearance (Genesis 3:24; Isaiah 6:6; Ezekiel 10:2; Daniel 10:6). The angels, when Jesus inherits His reign over all the earth, will serve Him and minister according to His will. And they will use what He has given them, or created them with, to do His bidding. Who the angels are and the fact that they will be doing things for the Lord is described poetically in this quote from Psalm 104:4. This is expressed also in Hebrews 1:14:

> Are they not all ministering spirits, sent out to render service for the sake of those who will inherit salvation? (Hebrews 1:14)

These angels minister or help those who will inherit salvation. Salvation, in the context of Hebrews, has a present reality where we experience what it means to know Jesus and partner with Him every day. This salvation has a future reality as well, in which how we live today will have an impact on how we will experience our companionship with Jesus forever. As I stated in the introduction, this is the main theme of the entire book.

Jesus will be King over all the earth; it is His inheritance, and no

---

[4] "The firstborn"—or the first to have risen from the dead to live forevermore (Romans 8:29; Colossians 1:15, 18).

one will stop that from becoming reality. Let me go up one verse to Hebrews 1:13:

> But to which of the angels has He ever said, "Sit at My right hand, until I make Your enemies a footstool for Your feet"? (Hebrews 1:13)

Because of who Jesus is and what He accomplished while here on earth, God the Father will give Him a land grant. It's as if God will say, in that future day, "The earth is yours." And Jesus will physically sit on His throne and reign over every corner of it. Everyone will bow to His Lordship.

The final thing that Hebrews 1 lays out as Jesus's inheritance is the theme of the entire book. Jesus will inherit the joy of companionship.

> "You have loved righteousness and hated lawlessness; therefore God, Your God, has anointed You with the oil of gladness above Your companions." (Hebrews 1:9)

The Greek word for "companions" is *metochos* ("meta-kos"), or *metochoi* ("meta-koi" in the plural); it means "those who are sharing or participating in the same thing." This word appears six times in the New Testament; five of those occurrences are in the book of Hebrews (Luke 5:7 is the only other). This word is the thread that holds the book of Hebrews together. Jesus has made it possible for us to be His companions, sharing in what He is all about, united with Him and His mission. We now can walk side by side with Him. And when we do, He experiences "the oil of gladness." This experience for Jesus can be felt to a degree now and will be felt to its fullest in the future kingdom.

When I was in college, my wife and I led a short-term mission trip to Southern California. We went to serve with World Impact, a mission organization that works with children through the inner-city Christian schools they've started. We actually worked at a camp sixty-five miles north of Los Angeles that World Impact owns called the Oaks. While we were there, we cut fire lines around the camp.[5] In our

---

[5] Fire lines: swaths of land where the brush and trees have been cleared to prevent a forest or brush fire from reaching camp by giving it nothing to burn.

group, most of us worked hard together, yet there were others who just goofed around. All of us were on the same trip, and most of us were partnering with each other. However, others were on the trip with us, but they were not working alongside us. Those who did not pitch in were not partnering in the mission and caused only frustration and disappointment. Those who shared in the mission had a great time together and experienced joy. As Christians, we can choose to just goof around or to join Jesus in His mission. If we choose not to partner with Jesus, it will cause frustration and disappointment in His heart (Matthew 25:26–28). But if we choose to be His companions, His *metochoi*, we will cause Him to experience the "oil of gladness," the joy of companionship. Throughout the whole book of Hebrews we find out how to be His companions.

As I mentioned above, in order to be Christ's companions we have to get to know Him. So after the first description of Jesus—He is an "heir"—a second description of Jesus is given: He is the Creator, as described in verse 2.

> in these last days has spoken to us in His Son, whom He appointed heir of all things, *through whom also He made the world.* (Hebrews 1:2)

Over and over again throughout the Bible, it states that Jesus created all things. Continuing to quote the Old Testament (Psalm 102:25) while describing who Jesus is, the author of Hebrews confirms this truth again down in Hebrews 1:10.

> And, "You, Lord, in the beginning laid the foundation of the earth, and the heavens are the works of Your hands… (Hebrews 1:10)

If Jesus created everything, and He created you and me, wouldn't we want to partner with our Creator? Especially since His purpose for creating us was to be His companions? If that alone does not convince us to walk with Him, how about this third description in verse 3: Jesus is God!

> And He is the radiance of His glory and the exact representation of His nature… (Hebrews 1:3a)

One Christmas, my daughter, Bethany, received some Play-Doh. I'm glad she got it, because I like to play with Play-Doh too. You can grab a big clump of it, hold it in one hand, and then press your fist into it. When you pull your fist out and look at the Play-Doh, you can see an exact imprint of your fist, right down to the cracks in your knuckles. In reading Hebrews 1:3 you might say that this doesn't imply that Jesus is God. You might say that it indicates that He is just the image of God, or the imprint of God, like the imprint of your fist in Play-Doh. But that verse is in fact saying that He is God, and to support it, the author of Hebrews quotes Psalm 45:6 in Hebrews 1:8:

> But *of the Son* He says, "Your throne, *O God*, is forever and ever, and the righteous scepter is the scepter of His kingdom. (Hebrews 1:8)

That verse has got to be one of the clearest and most pointed statements in the Bible that declares Jesus is God!

There are a *gazillion* images and opinions of who God is. But Jesus proclaimed it Himself, as recorded in John 14:9, when He said to Philip, "He who has seen Me has seen the Father." If we want to know God, we must get to know Jesus. If we want to walk with God, we must walk with Jesus—for Jesus and the Father are one.

The fourth description that Hebrews 1 lays out about Jesus (reminder: the first three are heir, Creator, and God) is He is the sustainer. As God, not only does He create, but also He sustains all things. If He did not hold this world and everything in it together, they would cease to exist.

> And He is the radiance of His glory and the exact representation of His nature, *and upholds all things by the word of His power.* (Hebrews 1:3)

That word, "upholds," is the Greek word *phero*. It is a verb, and it is important to know that it is a present active participle—a continuous action in the present. It means to carry, or to lift and carry along. Jesus sustains all things, carrying them along to His desired destiny. Continuing to quote Psalm 102:26–27, the author speaks of the earth and the heavens as He elaborates on verse 3. Jump down to verses 11–12:

> "They will perish, but You remain; and they all will become old like a garment, and like a mantle You will roll them up; like a garment they will

also be changed. But You are the same, and Your years will not come to an end." (Hebrews 1:11–12)

My grandma on my mom's side died in 2006, in Ashtabula, Ohio. My brothers and sisters (and their families), my mom and dad, my aunt and uncle and cousins, all met at my grandma's home before the funeral. My grandma had lived there her whole adult life, my mom grew up there with her sister, and we would go there often as grandkids. But when I got to her house that day, it felt strange. My grandma was gone, and now the house she had lived in for decades felt empty, like it had no purpose. It had been a great place for my mom to grow up in and for us to visit. The house was full of memories, but now that my grandma was gone, even though we were all there, it felt like we were inside of a huge void—like it had served us well, but its time was over.

The earth is very similar. It is serving a purpose: to teem with life (Isaiah 45:18), be a place for us to grow up in and enjoy great memories with the Lord and how amazing He is. Yet once all those who will come to the Lord and put their faith in Him as their Savior have done so and the Lord's glory is clearly acknowledged by all, this place will have served its purpose, and the world, as we know it, will perish (Matthew 24:14ff.;[6] 2 Peter 3:9–13). "Like a garment they will also be changed" by the Lord Jesus Himself into a new earth and new heavens. Until then Jesus sustains all things, carrying them along to His desired destiny.

The fifth and final description of Jesus in Hebrews 1 characterizes Him as a purifier (again, the first four are heir, Creator, God, and sustainer).

And He is the radiance of His glory and the exact representation of His nature, and upholds all things by the word of His power. *When He had made purification of sins*, He sat down at the right hand of the Majesty on high… (Hebrews 1:3)

I like being out in nature. I've enjoyed hiking in the Porcupine

---

[6] The abbreviation "ff." means "and the following for which an undetermined number of verses can be usefully given."

Mountains in Michigan's upper peninsula. It is a beautiful state park along the shores of Lake Superior. One of the men who went with me one year brought his SweetWater Purifier System, a small handheld pump that filters out 99.9999 percent of all waterborne bacteria. It took dirty water and made it pure, filtering out all those things that would have caused us harm. I like that word, "purification" (Hebrews 1:3). Jesus cleanses us—purifies us from our filth; He purifies us from our biting words that we use to cut people with and our impure or unfaithful thoughts or actions. Jesus purifies us from our selfish desires and our self-protecting dysfunctions. Jesus died to pay the penalty not for 99.9999 percent of all of our sin, but for 100 percent! By His death, He took what is dirty (our sin nature) and made it pure, so that nothing would get between us and the Lord. He did it so we could be His companions.

To know what being companions with Jesus looks like, to know how to walk with Him in a partnership relationship, the first step is to know who He is. And Hebrews 1 has spelled that out for us. Jesus is the (1) heir of all things, He is the (2) Creator of all things, He is (3) God, He is the (4) sustainer of all things, and He (5) purifies us from all our sins.

Do we want to be His companions? Do we want to partner with Him in this life as we look forward to partnering with Him to the fullest measure in the life to come? For me (and I hope for you) the answer is "Yes, knowing who He is, I want to be Christ's companion."

CHAPTER TWO

AVOIDING THE BLAHS

Hebrews 2:1–8

I live in Wisconsin. When I first worked on this section of the book of Hebrews, it was the middle of January. There was about ten inches of snow on the ground, and I remember thinking, *Two months ago we were heading into winter, and we have about two more months before we head out.* In the long season of winter, typically most days are cloudy, the temperature rarely goes above 25 degrees Fahrenheit, and we are forced to stay inside. Day after day it's hard to avoid the "blahs"—the winter blahs. Winter isn't the only thing we can feel "blah" about: a new job can start out fresh and exciting and then become routine; a new boyfriend or girlfriend can no longer seem interesting; a new marriage can become dull; a new hobby can become boring. Even our relationship with Christ can lose its vibrancy, its excitement. How can we avoid having the dust settle on our journey toward our eternal life? How can we avoid the "blahs" in our Christianity?

I've labeled this first part of the book of Hebrews "The Greatness of Glory" (Hebrews 1:1–5:10). As Christians, we are promised a future glory when we go to be with the Lord in heaven. And we can experience some measure of that future glory even now. We will see, as we look into Hebrews 2:1–8, that our Christian walk is not meant to be boring, routine, or dull in any way—at any time! This next section tells us how to avoid the blahs and gives us guidance so our life in Christ—right now—will be dynamic.

The first thing we see as we begin Hebrews 2 is we are commanded to keep intensely devoted to God's will.

> For this reason we must pay much closer attention to what we have heard... (Hebrews 2:1a)

"Pay much closer attention" or "to a much greater degree, pay attention," or "devote ourselves"—they all mean we are to heed what we hear. What this passage tells us is we must always be learning, growing, challenging our minds, and keeping a sharp edge "to what we have heard." Notice the concept of hearing. Many scholars believe this letter was actually a sermon that was preached. That is why it emphasizes listening. The sermon was written down and distributed to the new Christians who were primarily Jewish. Hence, the title of the biblical book is "The Letter to the Hebrews."

As has been practiced since the inception of the church, God's Word is preached to Christians. The author of Hebrews says, when God's Word is preached, we must listen. To really listen means we keep intensely focused to understand God's will for our lives, expecting to be changed. And the author tells us why in the first three words of Hebrews 2:1:

> *For this reason* we must pay much closer attention to what we have heard... (Hebrews 2:1)

For what reason? The reasons laid out in chapter 1. If I were to sum up what Hebrews 1 said, it would be thusly: Jesus is King—with a capital *K*. God spelled out His will through His Son (Hebrews 1:1–2), and all of chapter 1 explains Jesus as God—far above the angels; He will one day rule and reign with His companions (His faithful followers); and all His enemies will be made a footstool for His feet. Because all this is true and will come to be, we ought not be flippant in our devotion to learning and growing in our understanding of God's will for our lives today; we must not become blah—"we must pay much closer attention"!

The reality is, this is easier said than done. It's difficult to pay attention because we are *drifters*. It is our tendency not to stay focused.

For this reason we must pay mu(
heard, *so that we do not drift away*

If you put a piece of tape on a b
poke a pinhole into the balloo
not pop. Actually it will appea
to the balloon. However, slow
of the balloon. Initially, nothi
still floats, it still keeps its sh
begin to drop and shrink, an
air and will be lying on the
losing its air is an apt picture of how we end up
our walk with Christ. We don't wake up in the morning and say,
"I'm going to stop my relationship with Jesus today! It's done—
over!" No, it's always a slow drift.

One of my best college friends called me out of the blue and asked
if he could come over and talk. That wouldn't seem like anything
unusual, except for the fact that he lived in Iowa, and I was living in
Illinois at the time (which was at least an eight hour drive away). I said
to him, "Like now? Where are you?" He answered, "Yeah, I'm about a
hundred miles away and I need to talk. Can I come over?" I told him
of course he could come over. When I hung up the phone, I knew
something was wrong with his marriage. Jill and I were married when
I was in college, and this friend of mine was married too. Actually, our
weddings were on the same day. We hung out and had fun with each
other as couples. In our college days my friend and his wife seemed
to have a great marriage. So I wondered what he was going to tell us
when he got to our house.

When he arrived, it became clear, "We're done. It's over," he said.
When I asked him what happened, he said they just stopped spending
quality time with each other: she would do her thing, and he would
do his; she'd hang out with her friends, and he would hang out with
his.

There was an issue in his life I had warned him about for years:
I told him he must stop flirting with other women. He used to tell
me, "That's just who I am. It's not serious; I'm just having a little fun."
And then there were the little lies that crept in: not being completely

was or what he was doing. He'd say things like, be mad, so I didn't tell her what I was doing." And, mmed it all up by saying, "We just drifted apart."

rift—it's the same way with the Lord. We stop spending he with Him; we flirt with things that hurt our relationship m (maybe even giving ourselves the excuse that it's just who e or we are just having a little fun); we begin to believe the lies sin and even tell ourselves that we are not going to be honest and admit our faults to Jesus because He's just going to be mad. And slowly but surely we drift away from the Lord. The relationship that was once so vibrant and alive becomes blah.

That is not what God wants for us. He wants us to know the greatness of His glory! He wants us to experience a dynamic Christian life. He wants us to walk side by side with Him as His companions. So we need to understand that if we neglect our relationship with Him, He will correct us.

> For if the word spoken through angels proved unalterable, and every transgression and disobedience received a just penalty, how will we escape if we neglect so great a salvation? (Hebrews 2:2–3a)

This is the first of five warnings the book of Hebrews lays out. Notice the personal pronoun "we." The author includes himself. It appears as though Christians (even leaders like the author) will experience "a just penalty" if we neglect our great salvation. That word, "penalty," appears three times in the Bible: here and in Hebrews 10:35 and 11:26.[7] When we read the context of the other two references, we see that this word is used to describe what will happen at a future time when we, as Christians, will stand before the Lord and either be rewarded [for not shrinking back in our relationship and companionship with Him (not drifting away and enduring in the faith until the end)] or reprimanded by God [for neglecting our salvation] when we stand before Him in glory.

---

[7] "Penalty"—**μισθαποδοσία** (*misthapodosia*) *reward* Hb 10:35; 11:26; *punishment, penalty* 2:2.* [μισθός (*misthos*) (payment due for labor—wages, reward)+ ἀποδίδωμι (*apodidomi*) (fulfilling an obligation or expectation—to give, give back, pay back)] (Gingrich and Danker, *Greek-English Lexicon*).

He won't cast Christians[8] away from Him (sending them to hell); however, He will castigate or communicate firmly to them how they were wrong. This will result in a loss or forfeiture of eternal rewards. In the broader context of the book of Hebrews this "just penalty" can also refer to God's correction right now, for God disciplines us as His children (Hebrews 12).

When I first came to the church I am currently serving, the superintendent of our district in our denomination came and presented to me a shepherd's staff. Before the congregation he exhorted me to shepherd the flock that God had put under my care (1 Peter 5:1–2). That staff is in my office as a constant reminder to me of what a shepherd does. Our Lord is called the great Shepherd (Hebrews 13:20), and like a shepherd with actual sheep, He will nudge us, prod us, and sometimes even swat us if we need to be corrected. Ultimately, when we stand before His judgment seat, He will purify us through the fire of His "just penalty," His righteous correction. What He will be doing in that moment is cleansing us from how we have neglected this great salvation that He has provided.

Therefore, we ought never to take our salvation lightly. We must never be flippant about it. The next six verses will tell us why. First, our salvation links us to our forefathers.

> how will we escape if we neglect so great a salvation? After it was at the first spoken through the Lord, it was confirmed to us by those who heard, (Hebrews 2:3)

From the second half of this verse we learn that the author and those he was communicating to through this letter/sermon were one step removed from hearing the message of salvation directly from the Lord Jesus. A chain was beginning to be made that started with the Son of God, the Lord (Hebrews 1:1–2; 2:3). The first link was with His apostles and those disciples who followed Him while He was on the earth: "those who heard." They, in turn, took the truth from the Lord Jesus and handed it down to the next generation who was the speaker/writer of the book of Hebrews.

---

[8] Because we are His adopted children; cf. John 1:12; Romans 8:15–17; Galatians 3:26; Ephesians 1:5–6.

He then passed it on to the next generation—the recipients of this sermon/letter to the Hebrews. And this chain has been linked all the way down to us, one generation after another throughout church history.

You do not have to read too much history to know that the preservation of the purity of this chain, the truth of God and His will, and the gospel of salvation is nothing short of a miracle of God.[9] The purity of God's truth has been attacked from the beginning, but God has preserved it.

> God also testifying with them, both by signs and wonders and by various miracles and by gifts of the Holy Spirit according to His own will. (Hebrews 2:4)

This may have reference to the time when Jesus sent out His twelve disciples to proclaim the kingdom of God. At that moment He gave them power and authority over all the demons and to heal diseases (Luke 9:1–2). One chapter later, in Luke 10, we read that Jesus sent out the seventy to bring in the harvest of souls. They too were given authority to heal the sick, and they reported how "even the demons are subject to us in Your name." (Luke 10:1–17). Also, we can see from the book of Acts that God's power had accompanied the proclamation of the gospel through Peter (Acts 5:14–15; 9:32–41) and Paul (Acts 20:9–12). No matter how the author of Hebrews saw God's miraculous power while hearing the truth, one thing is clear: this unbroken chain of proclaiming God's truth is unexplainable apart from God Himself.

The present participle (rendered "while God endorsed" [NASB, "God also testifying"]) implies that the corroborative evidence was not confined to the initial act of preaching, but continued to be displayed within the life of the community.[10]

God bore witness then, and throughout the history of the church, that the Bible, which is taught and preached, is endorsed by Him because it is the proclamation of *His* truth.

So it is clear our salvation links us to our forefathers. Our salvation

---

[9] BILD International's course on "Essentials of Sound Doctrine."

[10] Lane, *Hebrews 1–8*, 47A, S. 39.

also calls us to carry the light of God's truth about our salvation today to our world. That is why the author of Hebrews tells us not to "neglect" our great salvation (Hebrews 2:3a). And like God did then, He still does today: He still accompanies the proclamation of salvation with the miracle of changed lives (Hebrews 2:4). People who were empty inside now know the love of the Lord; marriages have been healed by putting Jesus in the center of them; foul mouths have been cleansed when they are submitted to Jesus; and people who were drug users no longer want to take a hit because the Lord Jesus has become their satisfaction; and on and on the stories can be told of lives being changed because of the Lord saving people and by His Spirit living in them.

Another miracle of God that accompanies our salvation is He continues to give "gifts of the Holy Spirit according to His own will" (Hebrews 2:4) to make the church healthy and strong. I was talking with an elder in our church about how many Christians understand how God has gifted them. We agreed that the percentage is probably quite small of those Christians who know what their spiritual gifts are and who are using them to join with the rest of the church body to carry out the mission (Matthew 28:19–20). It is clear from the Bible that every one of us, as God's children and members of His church, are to use our spiritual gifts to make the church healthy and strong (Romans 12:3–13; 1 Corinthians 12:1–31; Ephesians 4:11–16). We can find out what our spiritual gifts are through serving the local church. As we serve, we learn more and more about how God has made us unique in our abilities to contribute to the proclamation of God's truth, to help others live according to His will, and to help others not neglect His great salvation.

You may not have a clear understanding of how God has gifted you. I would recommend that, in addition to serving, you find a test or worksheet that will help you understand what your spiritual gifts may be (ask a mature Christian leader in your church for a suggestion).[11] After taking the spiritual-gifts test, go to a trusted godly leader in your

---

[11] My advice would be to take a basic test (i.e., no more than fifty to one hundred questions) that will begin to help you understand how God has gifted you.

church and share with that person what you have discovered. Then ask that leader how you might be of service to help the local church become strong. All of us are responsible not to neglect our roles in this great salvation that God has given us.

So we do not neglect our salvation, because it connects us to the past, gives us responsibility in the present, and furthermore, it prepares us for our future. The author of Hebrews tells us that we have a destiny.

> For He did not subject to angels the world to come, concerning which we are speaking. But one has testified somewhere,[12] saying, "What is man, that You remember him? Or the son of man, that You are concerned about him? You have made him for a little while lower than the angels;[13] you have crowned him with glory and honor, and have appointed him over the works of Your hands; You have put all things in subjection under his feet." For in subjecting all things to him, He left nothing that is not subject to him. (Hebrews 2:5–8a)

---

[12] I have translated this as "Somewhere someone solemnly testifies saying" – διεμαρτύρατο δέ πού τις λέγων, or "Somewhere someone has testified, saying." The reason it seems so vague is for two reasons: (1) the author may very well have heard Psalm 8 preached by someone else (given the emphasis on the spoken word throughout Hebrews; (2) "chapter and verse" as we know them today, were not added until the 1500s. According to Aland, et al, *Greek New Testament*, xi. Stephanus put the numbers into the New Testament in 1551. And the Old Testament numberings evolved over time whereby circa 1528 we had the numberings pretty close to what we have today. So the author of Hebrews didn't have a specific reference location.

[13] There is a discrepancy in the quote from Psalm 8:5. Here, as well as in the original Greek, we see the word "angels." Psalm 8:5 (where this quote comes from) in the NASB reads, "Yet You have made him a little lower than *God*, and You crown him with glory and majesty!" The Hebrew word is מֵאֱלֹהִים, "elohim" (which is mostly translated "God" or "a god." However, it can be translated "rulers, judges, or divine ones—superhuman beings including God and/or angels, as the Brown-Drivers-Briggs Lexicon spells out. Yet the LXX (i.e., Septuagint, Greek translation of the Old Testament) translation is ἄγγελος, "angelos" (angels in the plural). Throughout the book of Hebrews the author quotes the LXX rather than the original Hebrew Old Testament.

Contrary to what some scholars believe (such as Zane Hodges)[14] this is not speaking about Jesus, this is speaking about "man" (verse 6), as in mankind—you and me. The flow of the passage indicates that this is still speaking about us. There is a transition in verse 9 where Jesus is brought into the picture. However, He is mentioned here for His role in making our future destiny possible. Hebrews 2:6–8a is a quote from Psalm 8, which also speaks about mankind.

Human beings were created to have dominion—delegated authority by God over His creation (Genesis 1:26, 28). This role we were made for was ruined[15] in the Garden of Eden when Adam and Eve ate the forbidden fruit (Genesis 3:1–19; 9:2—after the Flood, animals ran from us; they didn't follow our leadership). But God has not forgotten why we were made, and our destiny will be restored someday.

> "You have put all things in subjection under his feet." For in subjecting all things to him, He left nothing that is not subject to him. *But now we do not yet see all things subjected to him.*" (Hebrews 2:8)

I know the kingdom hasn't come yet. I know we are not experiencing what we were created to experience: to have dominion over creation, where all things would be in subjection to us. But this day is coming, and it is to be our focus for our lives even today. If we go to Psalm 8, where this passage (Hebrews 2:6–8a) quotes from, we will see what it is that we will have dominion over:

> What is man that You take thought of him, and the son of man that You care for him? Yet You have made him a little lower than God,[16] and You crown him with glory and majesty! You make him to rule over the works of Your hands; You have put all things under his feet, all sheep and oxen, and also the beasts of the field, the birds of the

---

[14] "A portion of Psalm 8 was now quoted. While the psalm as a whole is often read as a general statement about the role of man in God's Creation, it is clear in the light of Hebrews 2:5 and the application that follows in verses 8b–9 that the author of Hebrews read it primarily as messianic and eschatological" (Zane C. Hodges, in Walvoord and Zuck, *Bible Knowledge,* 784).

[15] It was ruined, damaged; however, it was not completely destroyed.

[16] See footnote 13.

heavens and the fish of the sea, whatever passes through the paths of
the seas. O Lᴏʀᴅ, our Lord, how majestic is Your name in all the earth!
(Psalm 8:4–9)

Yes, I think we are going to have animals in the world to come.
Not only do we see them mentioned here (and in conjunction
with our passage in Hebrews 2:6–8, this is speaking of a future
experience), but in the creation account, animals were made
before the Fall.

I know this role we are supposed to play has not happened yet
because of my four-year-old basset hound named Lucy. She is really
cute, but I read somewhere that basset hounds are bred to be stubborn
so that they don't give up when they are tracking down rabbits. I can
tell you that is true. She is a very loving dog. I wouldn't trade her
for any other dog. But she reminds me that I don't have dominion
over her. The other day she peed on the carpet in our bedroom. She's
four—well beyond potty training. I think she didn't want to go out in
the cold (this was January in Wisconsin). I was so mad. I mean, I've
spent time trying to train her and this is the respect I get? Of course
I was in the middle of studying this passage we have been talking
about here, and it reminded me that we are not in the kingdom yet.
If we were, she would have obeyed me all the time (maybe she would
have even been able to talk to me to tell me she had to go outside—
but that is sheer fun speculation on my part). The truth is if we were
in the kingdom, I would have been a better master. I hate to admit
it, but it was my fault. Lucy let me know that she was ready to go
outside, but I was slow to respond—too slow obviously. I picture a
day, in the kingdom to come and in the new world to come, when we
will know God's will and leadership in our lives, and from that we will
command the animals and they will listen. Not just the domesticated
animals but "the beasts of the fields, the birds of the heavens and the
fish of the sea, and whatever passes through the paths of the sea."
There will be perfect harmony.

In light of our eternity, how we live now matters: To have our
Christianity just be routine or dull or blah seems contrary to all that
it is about. The Lord saved us for a reason: to be the next link in the
chain, to carry the light of the faith, until the last link is attached—the
last generation, and then the end will come (as we know it); we will

be changed; His kingdom will be established. As we walk closely with God in faith, our awareness of His eternal plan increases. The more we know, the more in awe of this great salvation we become; the more exciting our lives become. In turn, the blahs are avoided and Jesus becomes our King with a capital *K*!

CHAPTER THREE

THE PERFECT

Hebrews 2:9–18

For seven years in a row I took a group of men up to the Boundary Waters Canoe Area in northern Minnesota. I called those excursions "Leadership Trips," because not only would we spend time in the woods, but we would intentionally talk about what it means to be a godly man and a godly leader.

Back in 2002, I went with five other men. A few days into the trip one of the guys, my friend Mike, was watching me get ready one morning, and he finally couldn't hold it in any longer. He blurted out, "Man, you are particular!" I asked, "What are you talking about?" He said, "You have to have your backpack packed just so; you pack the canoe a certain way; you put up and tear down the tent in the same sequence all the time. You're just very particular, that's all I'm saying."

Some people might label me "a perfectionist." I like to think of myself as someone who likes things done with excellence. Actually, my level of "particularity—perfection—excellence" depends on what I am doing. If I am constructing something, like doing some remodeling on my house, drawing a picture, packing my backpack, even preparing a sermon, then I am pretty particular. However (and you can verify this with my wife), putting my clothes away, keeping the bathroom spotless, and keeping the desk in my office clean are anything but perfection, even in the loosest sense of the word.

The reality is, those of us who want the things in our lives to be perfect need to realize that we just cannot have it that way. For *we* are not perfect. Only God is. Many of us work hard at trying to have our lives set up "just so." And we get frustrated because things don't go as we plan. But God works on a level that is perfect, because He is perfect. In this next section in the book of Hebrews we are going to see the perfect plan of God, and the perfect person by which this perfect plan centers on.

We now have arrived at Hebrews 2:9. In the perfect plan of God, the perfect person, Jesus, left the perfect place of the throne of God to pave the way for us to be with Him in glory. He left that glorious place to come to the earth in order to suffer and die. Then He went back up to glory after His resurrection.

> But we do see Him who was made for a little while lower than the angels, namely, Jesus, because of the suffering of death crowned with glory and honor, so that by the grace of God He might taste death for everyone. For it was fitting for Him, for whom are all things, and through whom are all things, in bringing many sons to glory, to perfect the author of their salvation through sufferings. (Hebrews 2:9–10)

The reason Jesus left His glory, came to the earth, and died was to give "everyone" (the last word in verse 9) the opportunity to be in glory with Him some day. In order for Him to die, Jesus was made for a little while lower than the angels. In other words, He was below them in splendor and majesty. Logically, this implies He came from a place where He was above them in splendor and majesty. This is confirmed in Philippians 2:5–8.

> Have this attitude in yourselves which was also in Christ Jesus, who, although He existed in the form of God, did not regard equality with God a thing to be grasped, but emptied Himself, taking the form of a bond-servant, and being made in the likeness of men. Being found in appearance as a man, He humbled Himself by becoming obedient to the point of death, even death on a cross. (Philippians 2:5–8)

Jesus was on His glorious throne in heaven, but He became a man. Therefore, He lowered His majestic appearance to the level of flesh and blood, lower than the angels. And He did this to carry out God's perfect plan. Notice the motivation behind the plan back in Hebrews 2:9:

> But we do see Him who was made for a little while lower than the angels, namely, Jesus, because of the suffering of death crowned with glory and honor, *so that by the grace of God* He might taste death for everyone. (Hebrews 2:9)

The motivation of this perfect plan has always been grace! God's perfect plan was propelled by grace. I love that word. The "grace of God" means God's infinite goodness to us even though we don't deserve it—and we can never earn it, ever!

I graduated from Phoenix Seminary in 1998. While I was there, I was working full-time as an operations manager for a distribution warehouse. We sold things like bouffant caps, polypropylene shoe covers, and latex gloves. One of our customers was TRW, who manufactured and assembled airbags for automobiles. They were working with a compound called sodium azide. It was a grainy powder that they pressed into the shape of a hockey puck (only smaller in size). That sodium azide was so combustible that you had to be careful even when you tied your shoes for fear that a tiny spark of static electricity would ignite the compound. Sodium azide is the substance that blows up the airbag in the event of a crash. The slightest little spark will transform this harmless-looking solid into an explosive gas: a chemical reaction transforming one thing into something totally different.

If we add one tiny spark of our works or behavior to why God gives us His goodness, we change His grace instantly into something totally different. It is no longer grace—it is something earned. Then grace explodes and is destroyed. God the Father sent His Son to taste death so that everyone can know His grace. Jesus was and is the perfect and only way for us to end up in glory with the Lord.

> For it was fitting for Him, for whom are all things, and through whom are all things, in bringing many sons to glory, to perfect the author of their salvation through sufferings. (Hebrews 2:10)

The plan that God has to bring many sons to glory—to bring us to be with him for eternity—was carried out in history when Jesus hung on the cross as the perfect sacrifice for our sin.

Notice Hebrews 2:10 says, "To perfect the author of their salvation through sufferings." This is not saying that Jesus became perfect in who He was, but it is saying that He became perfect in the role He was to play in this perfect plan. Jesus had to suffer and die in order to complete or perfect the only way that people could be with God in glory forever. He had to suffer and die in order to become the perfect Savior. By tasting death for everyone, He paid the perfect penalty for our sin.

Therefore, if you and I have trusted in Jesus alone for our hope of being in God's glory forever, then we have become united with Christ in a very deep and profound way.

> For both He who sanctifies and those who are sanctified are all from one Father; for which reason He is not ashamed to call them brethren, (Hebrews 2:11)

I call this the perfect union: Jesus considers us His brothers and sisters, "brethren." And notice the repeated verb: "sanctifies" and "sanctified." To sanctify means to set apart as holy, or to produce holiness in a person. Both uses in Hebrews 2:11 are present participles; one is in the active voice, and the other is in the passive voice. As present participles, both speak of a continuous action in the present. The verb that is in the active voice, "sanctifies," speaks of the one who is doing the action, and the verb in the passive voice, "sanctified," is the one to whom the action is being done. Jesus "sanctifies," and we are being "sanctified." We don't grow ourselves in holiness; Jesus is the One who purifies and cleanses us from the power of sin in our lives.

Being united with Jesus we can be sure that He wants to sanctify us in three areas. First, He wants to move us to be united with Him in having a heart full of gratitude and praise to God the Father.

> saying, "I will proclaim Your name to My brethren, in the midst of the congregation I will sing Your praise."[17] (Hebrews 2:12)

---

[17] Quoting Psalm 22:22.

This is about having an attitude of gratitude. Like this verse indicates, when Christians come together as a church, we are "the congregation." And when we gather, we sing songs of praise to God. We do this because we want to proclaim the name of Jesus and rejoice in our union with Him—our connection as brethren with Jesus.

Second, to sanctify us, Jesus wants us to trust God the Father as He does.

And again, "I will put My trust in Him."[18] (Hebrews 2:13a)

How is it that Jesus put His trust in God the Father? When Jesus became lower than the angels in order to carry out the perfect plan, He gave up acting independently and placed His trust and reliance upon God the Father. For example, Jesus trusted God the Father as He picked his twelve apostles (Luke 6:12); He trusted the Father in helping Him with His teachings (Matthew 14:23); and He also trusted God the Father with the care of His disciples when He was going to leave them after His death (John 17:9–11). At the time of His death, Jesus's trust in our heavenly Father was the most intense:

And Jesus, crying out with a loud voice, said, "Father, into Your hands I commit My spirit." Having said this, He breathed His last. (Luke 23:46)

The recipients of this letter[19] were Jewish people who were being persecuted for becoming Christians. Their lives were probably being threatened. The author was telling them in Hebrews 2:13, "Like Jesus, trust in God the Father. No matter what, even in the face of death, say to the Lord, 'Into your hands I commit my spirit, my soul, my life.'"

How are we doing at trusting the Father? How are we doing at placing our lives into His hands? Have we given up our independence so we do not act on our own initiative but seek to do His will? We are united with Jesus; therefore, we must put our trust in God the Father.

The third area that Jesus wants to sanctify is how we function as a

---

[18] Quoting Isaiah 8:17, "I will even look eagerly for Him."

[19] Or sermon in written form.

church family. The local church is a congregation; Jesus wants us to live like a family.

> And again, "Behold, I and the children whom God has given Me."[20] (Hebrews 2:13b)

The terms used are deliberate: "brethren" in Hebrews 2:11 and "children" in Hebrews 2:13 and again in 2:14. These are family or familial terms.[21] The number one analogy given in the Bible to describe the church is that of a family. It is challenging to be a healthy church family: relationships take effort, transparency, and honesty. Each church family must establish environments where we can practice loving one another. There is no such thing as a perfect family because, as we have established, being human means being perfect is impossible. Yet, under God's grace, a family stays healthy by giving each other grace. Also, we live in a world that has forces of evil and darkness (the devil and his demons) that are always waging war against the children of God (Matthew 16:18).

Even though we are not perfect and no church is perfect, God has provided a perfect plan, with a perfect union with Jesus. And Jesus dismantles the devil's weapons used for death and destruction:

> Therefore, since the children share in flesh and blood, He Himself likewise also partook of the same, that through death He might render powerless him who had the power of death, that is, the devil... (Hebrews 2:14)

The Bible is clear: a spiritual battle is constantly being waged (Ephesians 6:10–20), and it is Jesus who disarms the devil and takes his power away. One of the most powerful weapons of the devil is fear. Jesus sets us free from fear.

> Therefore, since the children share in flesh and blood, He Himself

---

[20] Quoting Isaiah 8:18.

[21] "The joining of the psalm passage with the one from Isaiah may be on the following basis. First, the *mou/moi* in the two passages quoted provided degree of verbal analogy, and these pronouns are closely related to the terms of family relationship in each of the respective passages (*adelphos/paidion*)" (Beale and Carson, *Commentary on the New Testament*, 949).

likewise also partook of the same, that through death He might render powerless him who had the power of death, that is, the devil, and might free those who through fear of death were subject to slavery all their lives. (Hebrews 2:14–15)

The recipients of this letter in the first century feared for their lives. "Often people make wrong moral choices out of their intense desire for self-preservation."[22] It is amazing how powerful fear is. Out of fear we will think, *I have to tell a lie or I might lose my job*, or, *I can't tell anyone because they might hurt me*, or, *I won't let people know me deeply because they will probably reject me*, or, *I can't admit it; I'll be in big trouble*. So, out of fear, we hide, lie, cover up, and clam up. Jesus came to set us free! He knows us fully (even how messed up we are), and He loves and accepts us unconditionally.

As Jesus taught in the temple, He looked around at the Jews. Knowing their hearts, and what drove them to disobey God (fear of rejection by other Jews, fear of the Roman Empire taking away their power, etc.), He said these words, "So if the Son makes you free, you will be free indeed" (John 8:36). If we are going to grow in being sanctified, we cannot live in fear. Jesus is near, and He is here to help us.

For assuredly He [Jesus] does not give help to angels, but He gives help to the descendant of Abraham. (Hebrews 2:16)[23]

And when we mess up, struggle, and sin, we must never forget that Jesus understands [firsthand] our imperfections.

Therefore, He had to be made like His brethren in all things, so that He might become a merciful and faithful high priest in things pertaining to God, to make propitiation for the sins of the people. (Hebrews 2:17)

To be the perfect sacrifice, Jesus had to become like us in every

---

[22] Walvoord and Zuck, *Bible Knowledge,* 2:785.

[23] The author was addressing the Jewish Christians who were the recipients of this letter; however, we too are Abraham's descendants according to Galatians 3:29.

way, except without sin. He did this so He could make "propitiation" for our sins.

To understand "propitiation," let me share a story from my childhood. Growing up, my younger brother had an uncanny ability to get under my skin. As a result, we would get into fights—physical fights. I was bigger than he was, and my parents would regularly step in and tell me that I must not beat up on my little brother. So I had an idea: I would make a punching bag and hang it out in the barn. My thought was, every time I got mad at my younger brother, I would march out to the barn and hit the punching bag. So I went out and got a feed sack and filled it mostly with straw but also with a little sand and hung it from the rafters. When I would get mad at my brother, I would let the punching bag have it. It helped. I didn't feel angry anymore after hitting the bag. That punching bag became the *propitiation* for my brother's sin. When Jesus hung on the cross, all the anger and the wrath of God against our sin were *punched* into His Son. Jesus satisfied the anger of God by taking our punishment upon Himself. That's what it means when it says that He made "propitiation for the sins of the people."

Hebrews 2 finishes with the truth that Jesus comes to our aid.

> For since He Himself was tempted in that which He has suffered, He is able to come to the aid of those who are tempted. (Hebrews 2:18)

In the context of this second half of Hebrews 2, the temptation that Jesus encountered when faced with the suffering that lay ahead for Him was, out of fear, the temptation to compromise. You may remember the struggle He had when He was in the Garden of Gethsemane. "And He withdrew from them about a stone's throw, and He knelt down and began to pray, saying, 'Father, if You are willing, remove this cup from Me'" (Luke 22:41–42). Jesus knew the plan from all of eternity past, and He knew His role. But He still had fear to the point where He was sweating drops of blood in His agony. And that fear led to the temptation of compromise. But what He said next showed that He overcame that fear and is now able to come to the aid of those of us who have the temptation to compromise. He said, "Yet not My will, but Yours be done" (Luke 22:42).

We are always tempted to compromise, especially when we fear. We can be honest and transparent and real with Jesus. He knows us, and He's been there. Call on Him. Say, "Lord, help me! Lord, I'm afraid, and I'm tempted to compromise in order to try to protect myself. But I am going to follow You. I can't do this without You. Help me. I'm not perfect, but I know You are. Carry out Your perfect plan in my life. Not my will but Yours be done."

Chapter Four

OUR HEAVENLY CALLING

Hebrews 3:1–19

For as long as I can remember I have been a Green Bay Packers fan. On February 6, 2011, the Green Bay Packers won the Super Bowl, and their quarterback Aaron Rodgers earned the MVP award. However, when they look back on that game, they will note that all the players on the team played their positions well. They all knew the role they were supposed to play, and they all understood their purpose to win the Super Bowl.

For most people, understanding the role we are to play—our purpose for why we are here—is not as easy and clear as an NFL football player understanding his purpose on the football field. If I were to tell you, "You have a higher calling, a higher purpose that has more dignity for you today and more reward for you in the future than any glory that the Super Bowl could ever offer to any football player," would you believe me? As we move into Hebrews 3, we will see that the author writes about our calling—our glorious calling—a "heavenly calling" that has the potential to be played out in each of our lives right now.

Hebrews 3 begins by telling us our heavenly calling is for us to be students—students of Jesus. We are called to be constantly learning and growing in our understanding of who Jesus is:

> Therefore, holy brethren, partakers of a heavenly calling, consider
> Jesus... (Hebrews 3:1a)

Christians, "holy brethren," are to "consider Jesus." The root of the
Greek word for "consider" is the word for "thinking" (*noeo*, **νοέω**).
Then there is a suffix added to the root, which intensifies it (*kata*,
κατα). The author of the book of Hebrews is telling us that a part of
our heavenly calling is to be deep thinkers when it comes to Jesus. We
are called to be not just trite or cliché, but engaged in learning about
Jesus.

When we think about Jesus, what words would we typically use
to describe Him? We may use words like "Messiah," "Savior," "Son of
God," or "the Christ." Two words that typically do not come to our
minds when we think about Jesus are descriptions here in Hebrews
3:1.

> Therefore, holy brethren, partakers of a heavenly calling, consider Jesus,
> the *Apostle* and *High Priest* of our confession; (Hebrews 3:1)

Normally, we do not think of Jesus as an apostle. We know the
twelve men who followed Jesus during His public ministry were
called apostles. Yet, here in the book of Hebrews, it is a title given
to Jesus. The word "apostle" means "a sent-out one." "Christ was
sent by God as his ambassador, representing God to man."[24] We
established in Hebrews 1 that Jesus is God and therefore He is the
perfect representative of God the Father (Hebrews 1:3). We also
know Jesus was sent out by the Father from other passages in the
New Testament (John 3:16; 1 John 4:9–10).

There is another description given to Jesus in Hebrews 3:1: He
is the "High Priest"; no one is higher than Him in His priestly
function. He represents us to God the Father and makes us right
in God's eyes. This description is elaborated on extensively in the
book of Hebrews and therefore will be elaborated on in the chapters
to come.

The author of Hebrews was well aware that the Jewish Christians
knew their people's history. Therefore, he recalled how God used

---

[24] Oberholtzer, "The Kingdom Rest," 186.

Moses, their past leader, to help them understand the role of Jesus. Jesus understood His purpose and calling, and He was faithful to His ministry.

> He [Jesus] was faithful to Him who appointed Him, as Moses also was in all His house. (Hebrews 3:2)

Jesus has been God the Father's representative—His ambassador—ever since He walked this earth, just like Moses was, fifteen hundred years before Jesus, or circa 1500 BC. The "house" that Moses was faithful to was the Jewish people as a whole who were rescued out of Egypt (Exodus 12–14). Numbering over one million, they came out from their slavery under the Egyptians and then wandered in the wilderness for forty years (Exodus-Deuteronomy).

> For He has been counted worthy of more glory than Moses, by just so much as the builder of the house has more honor than the house. For every house is built by someone, but the builder of all things is God. Now Moses was faithful in all His house as a servant, for a testimony of those things which were to be spoken later; (Hebrews 3:3–5)

What would be spoken of later would be a new house: the church, which would be born approximately fifteen hundred years later. Here is the point: just as God created the Israelites as a nation to be His house under Moses, God created the church to be His house under Christ.

> but Christ was faithful as a Son over His house—whose house we are, if we hold fast our confidence and the boast of our hope firm until the end. (Hebrews 3:6)

Another part of our heavenly calling is to be the church that God desires us to be. To become this church does not just happen passively. Notice again what the Hebrews author wrote in the second half of this verse: "if we hold fast our confidence and boast of our hope firm until the end." What, or who is our confidence and our hope? Our confidence and our hope is Jesus. To live out our heavenly calling as a church we must not just know *about* Christ, we must know Him personally as well. And that takes effort. To "hold fast our confidence…firm until the end" means we must work at it.

How do we know when we know someone? How can we know that we know Jesus? Maybe the best way to answer that is to think about a person in our life that we can say we know better than all others. For me, it's my wife, Jill. We have been married for over two decades, and the longer we know each other and invest in our relationship by talking and sharing life together, the more I know her and she knows me. I know we are on the same page relationally when I notice we are clicking with each other: we think the same way, we say the same things, we feel the same way, etc. A good marriage doesn't happen overnight; nor does it happen passively. A husband and a wife must continue to work at it, invest in it, and be committed to it. It's the same way with Jesus. Our relationship with Him has the potential to grow over time. However, the only way that it will grow is when we work at it, invest in it, and are committed to it.

In order to grow in our relationship with Jesus, one way we work at it is by listening to His voice. The author of Hebrews quotes the second half of Psalm 95 to make this point:

Therefore, just as the Holy Spirit says, "Today if you hear His voice, do not harden your hearts as when they provoked Me, as in the day of trial in the wilderness, where your fathers tried Me by testing Me, and saw My works for forty years. Therefore I was angry with this generation, and said, 'They always go astray in their heart, and they did not know My ways'; as I swore in My wrath, 'They shall not enter My rest.'" (Hebrews 3:7–11)

God led the Israelites in the wilderness for forty years. He showed them how He was working, and they still did not listen to Him. But we must! We need to listen to the voice of God. But how?

Some say, "It's that still, small voice in your heart that you have to listen to." They say that is the Holy Spirit speaking to you. The only place in the Bible where that phrase, "still small voice," is found is in 1 Kings 19:12 in the King James Version and the Revised Standard Version Bibles. The New American Standard Bible and the English Standard Version among others say "a gentle blowing" or "gentle whisper" or similar. The context of 1 Kings 19 is the scene where

Elijah the prophet fled from Jezebel and was feeling very alone. God found him in a cave, and the Lord passed by him and revealed His mighty power through a strong wind, an earthquake, and fire; although, God was not in any of them. After that there was "a sound of a gentle blowing" (New American Standard Bible). Or, it could be translated, "a still small voice" (King James Version). It is not conclusive this was actually the voice of God or if it was just a gentle wind blowing.

Another Old Testament passage people think about when they want to understand how to hear God's voice is found in Psalm 46:10: "Be still, and know that I am God: I will be exalted among the heathen, I will be exalted in the earth" (King James Version). Or in the New American Standard Bible it reads, "Cease striving and know that I am God; I will be exalted among the nations, I will be exalted in the earth." However, this verse says nothing about God speaking in our hearts. The point I'm trying to make is that we must be careful. Looking too inward or being too subjective or relying too much on our feelings when it comes to trying to hear the voice of God may not be the best way to hear Him.

One of the two primary ways the Bible says we hear the voice of God is through each other.[25] As brothers and sisters who are born again, we have the Holy Spirit living within us. God uses us to be His voice. This is a huge responsibility, not to be taken lightly, but it is true. The author of the book of Hebrews moves from the Israelites to the church today—God's people. He writes about how to avoid the hardening of our hearts and how to hear God's voice today (as the author said we could in Hebrews 3:7).

> Take care, brethren, that there not be in any one of you an evil, unbelieving heart that falls away from the living God. But encourage one another day after day, as long as it is still called "Today," so that none of you will be hardened by the deceitfulness of sin. (Hebrews 3:12–13)

Some people may not believe it, but Christians are susceptible

---

[25] The next chapter (Hebrews 4) will spell out the other way that we hear the voice of God: through the Bible (verses 12–13) joined with prayer (verses 14–16).

to having "an evil, unbelieving heart that falls away from the living God." We must encourage each other so this does not happen. Encouragement that packs a punch in a positive way pushes people toward the things of the Lord. Therefore, as encouragers, we must be honest, open, and honorable.

To be *honest* with our encouragement means we are not practicing flattery or being fake. We should not encourage others in order to manipulate them for our own gain; but, we are to speak the truth in love, being *open* about our own weaknesses. None of us have arrived yet (nor will we until we see Jesus face-to-face). Therefore, we encourage, not acting superior, but being open with our own struggles. And to be *honorable* means that we treat another person's weakness with dignity. As a church, we can create a safe environment where people who *have been hardened by the deceitfulness of sin* are loved unconditionally and are spurred on to love our living God well.

One more part of our heavenly calling that Hebrews 3 brings out is we are called to be companions with Jesus.

> For we have become partakers of Christ, if we hold fast the beginning of our assurance firm until the end… (Hebrews 3:14)

That word, "partakers," is a common word in the book of Hebrews. The word is *metochoi*, which means to be companions, comrades, or those who partner with Christ (see the explanation under Hebrews 1:9 in chapter 1). The only way that we can be partners, partakers, or companions with Jesus is if we hold tight to (or cling to) our assurance.

> For we have become partakers of Christ, *if we hold fast the beginning of our assurance firm until the end,* (Hebrews 3:14)

The word "assurance" is the objective truth that governs our reality as brothers and sisters in Christ and partakers of a heavenly calling. The foundation of who we are brings us right back to Jesus: He is our Rock, He's the One who has given us "so great a salvation" (Hebrews 2:3). We must never take our salvation for granted or treat it flippantly; we must hold it fast, cling to it, treat it with respect. To live up to our heavenly calling of being a companion of Jesus we have to keep believing in Him. Reflecting back on the Israelites in the wilderness, the writer of Hebrews quotes Psalm 95 again.

> while it is said, "Today if you hear His voice, do not harden your hearts, as when they provoked Me." For who provoked Him when they had heard? Indeed, did not all those who came out of Egypt led by Moses? And with whom was He angry for forty years? Was it not with those who sinned, whose bodies fell in the wilderness? And to whom did He swear that they would not enter His rest, but to those who were disobedient? So we see that they were not able to enter because of unbelief. (Hebrews 3:15–19)

Every single person who left Egypt had a right to enter the Promised Land, the land of Canaan where Israel is today. Even though God had miraculously delivered them from slavery in Egypt, fed them and protected them in the desert, they never really trusted God or Moses to lead them to their Promised Land. Therefore, of the over one million people who could have entered, only two did: Joshua and Caleb. What these two men had was a consistent faith in God and in His plan for their people. What the rest of the Israelites could have won was not a free gift like our salvation. It was dependent upon their believing in God consistently over the forty years they were in the wilderness. Likewise, our heavenly calling today is to have a consistent, persistent faith in our Lord: trusting in Him daily as we walk through the wilderness of our lives.

At the beginning of this chapter, I said that our calling is a bigger deal than an NFL football player's calling to win the Super Bowl. But that is not the way the world sees it. Those football players in the Super Bowl are superstars. When the Packers won, they came back to Green Bay and were honored by over seventy thousand fans in Lambeau Field, even though the temperature outside was in the single digits with the wind chill around -10 degrees. The Super Bowl was the most watched show ever in the history of television. According to the world, our heavenly calling is not greater than the calling of an NFL football player on Super Bowl Sunday. Yet we know the greatness of the glory of our heavenly calling has never been based on how many people think it's great, or how popular we are, or the fame that we have. The greatness of our glorious calling is based on God and His

Word—His absolute truth. He has told us all along that whether we are a businessperson, a high school student, a doctor, a lawyer, a homemaker, or even an NFL football player, God calls us to the same thing: to think deeply about His Son, to know Jesus personally, and to join Him in what He is doing in our world. There is nothing on earth that is a higher calling than that.

Chapter Five

GOD'S REST

Hebrews 4:1–16

I grew up in a home with eight siblings. So, leading up to every Christmas, my mom and dad had a challenge on their hands: hiding all the Christmas presents before Christmas morning. One year, because I had a curiosity that sometimes got the best of me, I went looking for my Christmas presents—and I found one. It was underneath my dad's desk in his den: a little cage with two little gerbils. I was so excited, but my mom and dad were angry that I had snooped around. My mom said to me that because I already saw my present maybe she would give those gerbils to one of my brothers or sisters instead of me. I pleaded with her, and I ended up getting them that Christmas. I liked those little guys. One thing I could never understand about them was why they would get on that little exercise wheel over and over again. I used to think, *What a waste of time.* They would run as fast as they possibly could and get nowhere. They would spin and spin and spin, faster and faster and faster, then stop, look around, and go back at it, day in and day out.

For most people in America we are a lot like those gerbils. I hear people say things like, "I need more sleep; I'm not getting enough. I can't get recharged." People talk about how they have to run their kids here and get them involved there. It is common for others to say how their jobs can be so demanding, so overwhelming. We as Christians add to the madness by including involvement in doing what God wants us to do in our communities and in our churches. Yet, all along, it's like we are on that little exercise wheel, just spinning and spinning and spinning, faster and faster and faster. I wonder if we are really getting anywhere?

Like my gerbils, we sometimes will stop and look around: It's called a retreat, a vacation, or some cool conference we will attend. But it's not long until we go right back at it. As a friend of mine once said, "We live in a culture of perpetual motion. We wear 'busy' as a badge of honor; activity equals worth; 'doing' has become our identity."[26]

I have observed that many of us are exhausted most of the time. I know I can get to a point where I find myself lying in bed at the end of the day wondering if this hectic pace will ever end. Will we ever slow down? We know there are passages in the Bible that speak about "rest" or "Sabbath," and we wonder if there will ever be a day when we will stop spinning and spinning, faster and faster. We ask ourselves, "Will there ever come a day when this madness will stop for good?" Dozing off, we wish that day would come soon…then the alarm goes off to pull us out of bed to go at it again.

God's rest—a place where we cease striving. It is an experience of peace, calm, quiet, or a stillness down in the depths of our souls. Is that place even possible? Do we have to wait for heaven before we can experience it? What is God's rest anyway? As we continue in our study through the book of Hebrews, chapter 4 will give us the answers.

In starting out the chapter, it seems as if God's rest *is* possible; but in order to experience it, we must choose it.

> Therefore, let us fear if, while a promise remains of entering His rest, any one of you may seem to have come short of it. (Hebrews 4:1)

Notice that the author, a Christian, includes himself, "let *us* fear." As Christians, what do we have to fear? According to this verse, we must fear that any one of us would come short of entering God's rest.

To understand God's rest and to know how to enter it, or not "come short of it," like everything else in life, we need to be taught. We need teachers, and we need to be teachable. The remainder of Hebrews 4

---

[26] See Todd Thompson's website, "Meltdown," www.asliceoflifetogo.com.

gives us directions so we have what we need in order to enter God's rest. One thing that we need is preaching the truth on this subject, and then we need to trust that truth and live in line with it. Or, as the author puts it, we must unite the hearing of this good news with faith, or believing. Then, we will enter God's rest.

> For indeed we have had good news preached to us, just as they also; but the word they heard did not profit them, because it was not united by faith in those who heard. For we who have believed enter that rest… (Hebrews 4:2–3)

Here the pronouns "they" and "those" refer to the author's illustration of the Israelites wandering in the wilderness for forty years (referred to in the previous chapter, Hebrews 3). They heard God's will and His truth through Moses, but it went in one ear and out the other. Therefore, it was of no profit because it was not coupled with faith. We must not only hear the preaching of God's truth, but we must believe God's proclaimed truth.

In this passage the author says "good news." This does not just mean the salvation message that Jesus died for our sins and rose again on the third day. It does not just mean talking about entrance into God's family. Beyond all that, it is also the good news of God's rest and how we can know it in our lives even now.

Looking forward to God's rest, we need to understand that it does not come through works, or through our good behavior.

> For we who have believed enter that rest, just as He has said, "As I swore in My wrath, they shall not enter My rest," although His works were finished from the foundation of the world. For He has said somewhere concerning the seventh day: "And God rested on the seventh day from all His works"; and again in this passage, "They shall not enter My rest." (Hebrews 4:3–5)

Back in high school I wanted to be buff. So I lifted weights. Honestly, I never really got into it. It was okay, but I felt like I was doing it just because I was supposed to. Back then my friends always wanted to know how much I could bench. So I would lie down on the bench press and try to get my personal best. My favorite part about lifting weights (and this will prove to you that I never really enjoyed weightlifting) was when the spotter, who stood at the head of the bench looking down at me, would stop shouting, grab the bar off my chest, and put it back on the rack for me. Some Christians, and preachers, think it's God's will to shout at people: "Come on! Shape up! Get going! You want to be a great Christian? You have to be intense! I want you in the weight room of doing the right thing all the time! Do this; don't do that!" And we do it because we're supposed to.

These Jewish Christians to whom Hebrews was addressed came out of that. They came out from under the Pharisees and the law. And no doubt, they were carrying that attitude into their Christianity. In Hebrews 4:3–5, the author wanted to communicate that God worked but now He rests. And if we add works so that we can know His rest, we will not enter it. You and I will not know God's rest by striving to obey the law or by keeping the "dos" and "don'ts." The author knew he had to lift the bar of the law off their chests and put it back on the rack.

> Therefore, since it remains for some to enter it, and those who formerly had good news preached to them failed to enter because of disobedience, (Hebrews 4:6)

That word, "disobedience," is the Greek word—ἀπείθεια (apeithea), which can also be understood as "obstinacy," being obstinate against God's will, or being stubborn to do things their own way; headstrong. The Israelites did not have the problem of being legalistic (like the recipients of the book of Hebrews probably had). Their problem was being headstrong, stubborn, obstinate. Being either legalistic or obstinate will destroy any hope of knowing God's rest.

> He again fixes a certain day, "Today," saying through David after so long a time just as has been said before, "Today if you hear His voice, do not harden your hearts." For if Joshua had given them rest, He would not have spoken of another day after that. So there remains a Sabbath rest for the people of God. (Hebrews 4:7–9)

"The people of God" refers to you and me as Christians. This passage adds a new word to the word "rest": "Sabbath." A Sabbath is really a counterbalance to the elements of life. In the wilderness the Israelites were to stop collecting manna and stop moving or working. On the Sabbath the Jewish people were to stop doing things.

In the Bible, farmers were to stop plowing or harvesting (Exodus 34:21); salespeople were to stop selling (Jeremiah 17:27); a sabbatical year was every seventh year where the land was to not be planted (Leviticus 25:1–7). It was the year of Jubilee marked by amnesty for slaves, debtors, and the dispossessed (Leviticus 25:8ff.).[27]

In our lives today the Sabbath means we stop spinning on the exercise wheel of life. We stop trying to make life into what you and I want it to be. We stop trying to fix life on our own terms. We S.T.O.P. We cease doing what we always do and get aligned with God so we can know Him and His rest. This "Sabbath rest" is available to us every day as we stop and connect with God. We don't work for it, but we must be diligent about entering it.

> For the one who has entered His rest has himself also rested from his works, as God did from His. Therefore let us be diligent to enter that rest, so that no one will fall, through following the same example of disobedience. (Hebrews 4:10–11)

Where we focus our diligence is the key to entering His rest. We must be diligent with God's Word and let it pierce our hearts and expose our thoughts. It is God's Word that God wants to use to transform us, mold us, and lead us into His rest.

> For the word of God is living and active and sharper than any two-edged sword, and piercing as far as the division of soul and spirit, of both joints and marrow, and able to judge the thoughts and intentions of the heart. And there is no creature hidden from His sight, but all things are open and laid bare to the eyes of Him with whom we have to do. (Hebrews 4:12–13)

Every Roman soldier had a double-edge sword on his hip. Each sword weighed between 2.5 to 3.5 pounds and was between 15 to 20 inches long. The soldiers were taught to thrust these swords rather than slashing them for maximum effect.

A thrust with the sword has penetrating power, whereas the slash, which often is difficult to aim and control, may strike a bone or the opponent shield and thus will do comparatively little damage. The

---

[27] Atkinson, Field, Holmes, O'Donovan, *New Dictionary*, 853.

thrust is delivered with strength of the entire body, while the slash is executed solely by the elevation of the right arm and carries the weight of the weapon.[28]

The main weapon for a soldier was a javelin or a spear. The sword was used only in close combat. Likewise, the Word of God is used for close combat. God uses it to pierce our hearts. Its purpose is not just to slash around with the knowledge we gain from it, but it is to be thrust deeply into our hearts in order to bring transformation. When our lives are spinning faster and faster and we can't seem to find an opportunity to stop and seek the Lord, it is really an issue of the heart. What is behind the busyness of life, the striving—the "doing"? It is the Word of God that can expose the answers and realign us with His will.

> And there is no creature hidden from His sight, but all things are open and laid bare to the eyes of Him with whom we have to do. (Hebrews 4:13)

The phrase "with whom we have to do" is tough to translate. Some translations say "to whom we must give an account." I don't think that is a good translation. The phrase, as best that I can decipher, means "the relation with whom toward us." As difficult as that is to translate, it appears that God uses His Word to expose the thoughts and the intentions of our hearts so that we can relate to Him better. That is what He is saying here: when we relate to Him better, in alignment with His Word, then we will know His rest.

God's rest is experiencing the mercy and the grace of Jesus as we draw near to Him. Through the proclamation of His Word (through preaching, teaching, and reading), the receiving of it, and then walking according to it by faith is how we will experience God's rest. To know Jesus in this life, to experience a relationship with Him, will happen only if we draw near to Him.

> Therefore, since we have a great high priest who has passed through the heavens, Jesus the Son of God, let us hold fast our confession. For we do not have a high priest who cannot sympathize with our weaknesses,

---

[28] McNab, *Roman Army*, 122.

but One who has been tempted in all things as we are, yet without sin. Therefore let us draw near with confidence to the throne of grace, so that we may receive mercy and find grace to help in time of need. (Hebrews 4:14–16)

That right there is a great description of God's rest: knowing God's well-timed help in our lives and experiencing His mercy and grace.

Recently I was talking to my friend Todd Thompson. He told me about a story from his past that he wrote about on his blog. The title of the story was "Still Waters."

It was a glorious summer day in late July 1978. I had spent the better part of an afternoon water skiing with my high school friends, Clair, Steve, Lori, and Kristi. A quintessential day for skiing, the water on Iowa Lake was calm, quiet and smooth as glass.

When the sun began to slip behind the trees lining the west side of the lake, we pulled in the ropes and turned the boat toward the dock. As we headed across the water I looked over at Clair and Steve and saw them putting their life jackets back on.

"Are we going to ski some more?" I asked.

Clair threw me a life jacket and said, *"Put this on."* Clair was two years older and bigger than I was, so I did. He then pointed at Kristi, *"You drive the boat."*

As Kristi took her place behind the wheel, Clair tightened the belt on his vest and said, *"Here's what we're gonna do. When Kristi gets this boat up to full speed, the three of us are going to jump out. It'll be fun."*

I believed him.

Kristi spun the boat around and jammed the accelerator forward. We were really flying. With a scream, Clair jumped over the edge. Then Steve jumped. Just like Navy commandos in a war film.

Then I jumped.

I hit the water, but I didn't go in the water. I just bounced and rolled across the top like dice on a card table. When I stopped rolling, I swooshed into the lake. After getting my bearings I looked around and saw Clair and Steve bobbing in the water like a couple of brainless buoys.

Somebody yelled, *"Is anybody dead?"*

Nobody was dead.

So we got back in the boat and did it again.[29]

In our fast and frantic pace of life, God's quiet waters, His rest, is available; but we don't know it by flying across it, or even getting out of our busy lives only to bounce and roll across His rest at lightning speed. We may end up bobbing up and down in God's rest, only to get back in the boat of our busy lives and fly across the top of it again.

The deep waters of God's rest can be known by us only if, according to Hebrews 4, we are diligent to know His rest. This abiding rest can be found only through swimming deep into His Word and letting it expose our hearts, and then drawing near to His Son, Jesus, our "great high priest." It is there we will see Him actively working and helping by pouring out His mercy and grace into our lives. If we would just take the time and stop—cease from the normal elements of our lives—and listen to the preaching, teaching, or reading of His Word and pray and draw near to Jesus, we would sense His rest. His rest that He desires for us is our knowing His mercy and His grace in our lives in His well-timed and deeper way.

---

[29] See Thompson, "Still Waters." www.asliceoflifetogo.com

CHAPTER SIX

OUR HIGH PRIEST

Hebrews 4:15–5:10

Recently I gave a challenge to our church body: Read the Bible for seven days straight, for no less than fifteen minutes each time. It was based on Hebrews 4:12–13—how God uses His Word to open up our hearts to reveal to us our thoughts and intentions and to draw us near to Him. The following Sunday I had to confess that I did only five of the seven days. I was the one who gave the challenge, and I couldn't even do it. Committing to disciplines that help our relationship with Jesus is tough to do.

It's not always easy living out this Christian life. The Bible doesn't *always* spell out right from wrong in *every* situation. For instance, I saw a movie with my son (who was nineteen) that I thought wasn't too bad. It did not have any nudity or any bad language. But then while talking to another Christian, the topic of that movie came up. She said how much God must be so angry that that movie was even made. She was adamant that Christians should boycott it. Honestly, I didn't tell her I saw it, but it made me wonder, did I sin?

As Christians, we can think we have reached some level of wisdom and then find ourselves in situations where we feel so unwise. We have to deal with pressures from so many angles: our bosses, our parents, our friends, society, etc., and we may end up choosing to do things that Jesus may not approve of.

Also as Christians, we know that Jesus died for our sins; for that we are thankful. But our relationship with Jesus isn't just about admiring Him for what He did for us on the cross, or even having enthusiasm for who He is. Christianity is not only about our intellectual or spiritual understanding, but it is also about spiritual experiences. In addition to our Christianity being objectively true (based on the Bible and the truths about Jesus), it is also experiential. Our Christianity is about practical events either internal or external that we know have come about because we have a relationship with Jesus. Our Christianity is built on knowing Jesus has done something in our lives. For example, our Christianity is not just what the Bible says about having victory in Jesus (or even singing a song with that phrase as its title), but it is also about experiencing real and practical victory, which Jesus has brought about in our lives.

The book of Hebrews calls Jesus our high priest, and it indicates that He is near to help us as we draw near to Him.

> For we do not have a high priest who cannot sympathize with our weaknesses, but One who has been tempted in all things as we are, yet without sin. Therefore let us draw near with confidence to the throne of grace, so that we may receive mercy and find grace to help in time of need. (Hebrews 4:15–16)

From the first recipients of this letter all the way through the ages of church history, I imagine that those who have heard or read those words have asked, "How is it that Jesus helps us? How is it that we receive mercy and find grace? And tangibly speaking, what is the role that Jesus plays in our lives today as our high priest?" To answer these types of questions, the author of Hebrews used an illustration that the first recipients of this letter would all understand. Remember: the readers were Jewish Christians—they came out of Judaism. Therefore, they knew Jewish history and the role the high priest had played in the temple. So the author pointed them to the role of the high priest during the time of Moses when the Israelites wandered in the wilderness.[30] The high priest was appointed by God to be the

---

[30] At that time the Israelites had a tabernacle (a temple in tent form so it could be portable as they wandered).

Israelites' helper before Him, helping them in their relationship with
God and in their worship of Him.

> For every high priest taken from among men is appointed on behalf
> of men in things pertaining to God, in order to offer both gifts and
> sacrifices for sins; (Hebrews 5:1)

When the Jewish people were in the wilderness, God called Moses
to establish the office of the priests (Exodus 28:1). The first one to fulfill
that office was Moses's brother, Aaron. Aaron and his sons carried out
the duties within the tabernacle, which included offering "both gifts
and sacrifices for sins." Of all the priests one was above them all; he
was the high priest. He was the only one who could actually make
the sacrifice of an animal that was acceptable as the payment for the
sins of all the people. He did this once a year on what was called the
"Day of Atonement." Also, the high priest was the only one who could
inquire of the Lord to understand His will and His judgments. Then
what the high priest said in conjunction with them was to be obeyed
without question by the Israelites (Numbers 27:21). Ultimately the
high priest acted as the mediator between the Israelite people and
God (Exodus 28:29).[31]

To illustrate the high priestly ministry of Jesus, the author of
Hebrews continued to paint the picture of the high priest during the
time of Moses. The high priest was typically a man of compassion.

> he can deal gently with the ignorant and misguided, since he himself
> also is beset with weakness... (Hebrews 5:2)

A good high priest was one who was gentle. Notice why he was
gentle: "since he himself also is beset with weakness." He knew he
was weak too. It seems to be human nature for us to quickly form our
opinions when other people around us fail in some way. And typically
we then are bent toward passing judgment against them (sometimes
in pretty harsh manners). We have a tendency to form our opinions
prematurely, and we seem to have the ability to size up everybody else

---

[31] "When he [the high priest] carried the breastplate with the names of the
tribes inscribed thereon he acted as mediator between Israel and God (Ex
28:29)." (Evans et al., *International Standard Bible Encyclopedia*)

but struggle with sizing up ourselves. A good high priest understood himself well and knew he was beset with weaknesses.

Our neighbor planted some rosebushes around her house a couple of years ago. When they were small, they didn't really produce many roses, and nobody ever criticized them in that first year. And our neighbor kept watering them and nurturing them along. Last year they were still young and underdeveloped. They had some small bugs on them, and not all of the roses had opened up; but again, no one criticized them. We knew the stage of life those roses were at. We've been enjoying those young plants at every stage of their development, and this year we are looking forward to seeing those rosebushes looking better than ever.

A rosebush is a rosebush from the time it is a seedling through the time that it dies. All that time it is constantly in the process of maturing. In each stage it's all right as it is, and it is the job of the rosebush keeper to continue to nurture it and help it reach its fullest potential. Notice again Hebrews 5:2:

he can deal gently with the ignorant and misguided, since he himself also is beset with weakness; (Hebrews 5:2)

The high priest gently nurtured those who were *ignorant* (who just didn't know the truth yet) and *misguided* (who had been told lies or were living a lie). As long as people were not arrogant, not thumbing their noses at God, the high priest, like a skilled rosebush keeper, would act compassionately toward those he was helping before God. The high priest understood how the people, like himself, had not reached their full potential yet.

and because of it he is obligated to offer sacrifices for sins, as for the people, so also for himself. (Hebrews 5:3)

The high priest, who lived among the Israelites, understood that when he offered sacrifices for sins, he was no better than the next guy and he needed payment for his sins too. He never had the feeling of superiority. High priests were men of humility.

And no one takes the honor to himself, but receives it when he is called by God, even as Aaron was. (Hebrews 5:4)

The call to be the high priest was the utmost calling in all of Israel. Yet it required incredible humility. The man in this position not only understood his own weaknesses, but he also had a healthy dependence upon God who called him. He always kept before him the only reason he did what he did was because of God's gracious calling on his life and enablement in his life. Rightly, he felt he was less significant than the office that he held. He knew he didn't have all the knowledge, wisdom, insight, and strength needed to fulfill his calling, and therefore he was a humble servant.

In reverse order, the author of Hebrews showed how Jesus, as our high priest today, possesses the same qualities that the high priest had during the time of Moses. The description Hebrews gives him first of all is that he is a man of humility. Just like Aaron was called by God the Father to be the Israelites' first high priest, Jesus was called by God the Father to be our first *and only* high priest.

> So also Christ did not glorify Himself so as to become a high priest, but He who said to Him, "You are My Son, today I have begotten You"; just as He says also in another passage, "You are a priest forever according to the order of Melchizedek." (Hebrews 5:5–6)

Here the author of Hebrews quoted Psalm 2:7 and Psalm 110:4, underscoring both the divine Sonship of Jesus and how God the Father directly called Jesus to the priesthood. Who Melchizedek is will be elaborated on when we get to Hebrews 7. For now, let these verses sink in: Jesus, the Creator and King of the universe (Hebrews 1:10), has become a servant of you and me as Christians. He accepted the call that God the Father placed on Him: to be our high priest, to serve you and me today. It is a humility that I cannot fathom; can you? But it is true!

Jesus is also a man of compassion. See if you can pick up on His compassion in the next verse.

> In the days of His flesh, He offered up both prayers and supplications with loud crying and tears to the One able to save Him from death, and He was heard because of His piety. (Hebrews 5:7)

This translation says "from death." Actually it is better to understand it as "out of death" (Greek: *ek thanatou*; *ek* can be understood as "out of" or "from"). Jesus knew He had to die, for He said, "But for this purpose I came to this hour" (John 12:27). He came to die for the sins of the world. He came to die so that all people would be saveable. In His final prayer He said to the Father, "Into Your hands I commit My spirit" (Luke 23:46). What He was saying was, "As I go to the grave, You, Father, are the One who has the power to deliver Me from the state of being dead." Or, "You are the One who can rescue me *out of death*." But that wasn't His only prayer when He was "in the flesh" here on earth. He offered prayers and "supplications" (Hebrews 5:7) for His disciples, for the lost, and even for you and me (John 17:20–26). And His feelings as He prayed are seen here in Hebrews 5:7, "with loud crying and tears." Jesus revealed His deep compassion for you and me in His prayers for us—He was a man of sorrows and acquainted with grief (Isaiah 53:3). His heart is for us—He wants us to know Him, to know the compassion He has for us. He cares for us with an infinite depth, and we can have a deep relationship with Him right now.[32]

> Although He was a Son, He learned obedience from the things which
> He suffered. (Hebrews 5:8)

How is it that the One who is perfect—sinless—learned obedience through His suffering? The best way that I know how to explain it comes from an experience I had when I was younger. Before I heard an orthopedic surgeon say that adults should not run, I used to run all the time. Now I have relegated myself to riding the stationary bike so I don't pound on my knees too hard. As a runner, sometimes I would go on long runs and push myself really hard. Periodically I would get what some call "runner's high." It was a feeling of euphoria, and the harder I ran, the better I felt. I can't really explain the sensation to you; I just felt like I was on top of the world. You can read about runner's high (something about a release of endorphins into our system), you can hear others describe it, but the only way for you to truly know what I'm explaining is if you get out there and reach that point where you experience it too.

Jesus had complete knowledge of all things, yet He learned what it meant to obey by becoming a man and living in this world that Satan

---

[32] Like the apostle Paul had (Philippians 3:9–10).

rules and sin governs. He endured extremely painful experiences, temptations, pressures, and therefore, *He learned obedience from the things which He suffered.* He did not learn *to* obey, for He has always had the perfect instinct in His sinless heart. But He learned *the nature* and *the benefit of* obedience as a man in our fallen world and how it positively affected drawing near to and knowing God the Father in real and tangible ways. Like becoming a runner and experiencing runner's high, Jesus became a man and experienced (learned) the euphoria of obeying the Father in this difficult world.

One more thing about Jesus being our high priest that this section of Hebrews 5 brings out: just like the high priests of the Old Testament, Jesus is our helper before God today.

> And having been made perfect, He became to all those who obey Him the source of eternal salvation, being designated by God as a high priest according to the order of Melchizedek. (Hebrews 5:9–10)

Here's another challenging verse: how can the One who is perfect become perfect? Jesus became perfect in that He carried out His ministry perfectly (to suffer and die for our sins). He could not be the perfect sacrifice for our sins without coming into our world and into humanity. Now that He has done that, He is our perfect high priest, our perfect helper before God.

In Hebrews 5:9, it appears that Jesus saves all of those who obey Him. "To all those who obey him" is literally "those who are obeying him." The verb is a continuous action in the present (a present participle). In the flow of the letter, chapters 3 and 4 spur us on to listen to the Lord's voice. The end of chapter 4 describes Jesus as our high priest who sympathizes with our weaknesses and calls us to draw near to Him. After the current section we are exploring, starting in 5:11, the warning is given not to become dull of hearing or sluggish (Hebrews 6:12). Before and after Hebrews 5:9, Hebrews is talking about sanctification, so it is only natural that the author is talking about sanctification here as well. The text is saying, for those who are obeying God right now, who are seeking to draw near to Him, and who want His help (Hebrews 4:16), He is "the source of eternal salvation."

Here again we must be careful to understand these words within the context and the flow of the chapter. When we read "eternal salvation," our minds may want to go directly to the thought of how we get to heaven: and if we obey Him now, if we draw near to Him consistently, if we are always close to Him and make sure we do not go away from Him, we can be sure of going to heaven to be with Him forever when we die. Is that what this is saying? No, I don't think so.

In our minds, when we read the word "eternal," we typically think only of time. However, "eternal" doesn't always speak of time. We can use that word in the place of "infinite." For instance, instead of saying, "God's attributes are infinite," we can say, "God's attributes are eternal." In this example, the word "eternal" is not speaking of time, but of God's characteristics. "Eternal" doesn't always mean that it extends beyond what we know as time. Eternal also means "infinitely beyond our comprehension." "Salvation" at its root means "deliverance" or "to be rescued." This is a salvation beyond our ability to perceive; it is a deliverance that is infinitely powerful.

What Hebrews 5:9 is saying is when we need to be rescued from the influence of sin in our lives, or we need help to grow in our faith, the power of Jesus inside of us has no limits! In the flow of the book of Hebrews, here we are talking about our experience with Jesus right now, not about something that will happen after we die.

If you and I are honest, we have to admit that we fail often. We are not consistent in our drawing near to Jesus. We struggle all the time with our relationship with the Lord: I couldn't make the challenge of reading the Bible seven days straight to invest in my relationship with the Lord that week. We find ourselves being tired, tempted, torn between loyalties; it's tough! But we have a high priest who is gentle, loving, and kind. He calls us to draw near to Him all the time, and in every situation. When we put our faith in His present, full, and eternal salvation in our lives today and turn to Him to experience His ever-ready help, we will find ourselves saying, "Yes, Jesus saved me years ago; but Jesus also saves me now. He is my helper and my high priest."

PART II

MATURING

Hebrews 5:11–6:20

CHAPTER SEVEN

FROM MILK TO MATURITY

Hebrews 5:11–6:3

We now enter into the second, and shortest, of the four parts that comprise Hebrews. It builds on what has been established in the first five and a half chapters and calls Christians to make sure they grow in their relationship with the Lord and in their responsibilities as Christians. This section also contains in it the most controversial passage of Hebrews (6:4–9), which has literally divided Christians along denominational lines. We will save the explanation of that passage for the next chapter. For now, let's look into Hebrews 5:11–6:3.

Just before Jesus ascended, He gave His disciples (and through them to the church for all generations) what is commonly called the "Great Commission." It is found in Matthew 28:19–20.

> Go therefore and make disciples of all the nations, baptizing them in the name of the Father and the Son and the Holy Spirit, teaching them to observe all that I commanded you; and lo, I am with you always, even to the end of the age. (Matthew 28:19–20)

These verses tell us—the church—why we exist. As Christians, it is a good practice to always evaluate how we are doing at this. How are we doing at helping people "to observe all that [the Lord has] commanded [us]"? How are we experiencing the truth that Jesus is with us always ("and lo, I am with you always")? This practice is vital to the Christian life because the church exists to make disciples and help Christians mature in Jesus.

Back in the days when the Roman Empire was fully mature and the church was in its infancy, the Romans celebrated almost everything. In any given year they had at least seventy-six public festivals.[33] In addition, Roman families had their own private festivals. One of those family festivals was celebrated to declare that a child had reached adulthood. For a boy, it was a holy day when he had his first shave. His whiskers were dedicated to a god.[34] The boy was typically given a white toga and a gift. The father would give a speech and then put the toga on his son. Then, for the wealthy, the gift the young man received would often be his very own slave.[35] From then on, the boy was considered a man and he was expected to act like one.

Identifying what it means to be mature is universal. Societies throughout the ages have had ways to acknowledge when children move into adulthood. In our American culture, we have things like movie ratings, the voting age, the age you can serve in the military, or when you can get a driver's license. As Christians, we talk about being mature, but how do we get there and what does it look like to be a mature Christian? This next section of the book of Hebrews (Hebrews 5:11–6:3) will help us find the answers.

The first thing we will see is we must be good listeners.

> Concerning him we have much to say, and it is hard to explain, since you have become dull of hearing. (Hebrews 5:11)

The translators of this verse had to make a decision. Our translation started this verse with "Concerning him." In the original language of the New Testament, which is Greek, these two words are "περὶ οὗ" (perri ou). "The relative pronoun οὗ could be understood as masculine ("him" or "whom"), referring to Melchizedek (in 5:10), though on balance it is preferable to take it as neuter ("this" or "which"), referring to Christ's priesthood (5:5–10 and chapters 7–10).

---

[33] Durant, *Story of Civilization*, 377–78.

[34] Durant, *Story of Civilization*, 372.

[35] Douglas, *Robe*, 3.

The expression indicates that the author was aware of the breadth of the subject.[36] The NIV, ESV, NLT, RSV[37] all translate οὗ as "this," in the neuter, referring to the priesthood of Jesus, not Melchizedek. That seems to fit the flow of the letter/sermon better.

In the expression περὶ οὗ it seems preferable to consider the relative pronoun οὗ as a neuter, having reference to the priesthood of Christ in its totality, rather than as a masculine relative, which has for its antecedent "Melchizedek" in v 10. It is the whole subject under discussion, and not simply the priesthood like Melchizedek's, that requires the skill of the writer and the attention of the community.[38]

So here is the conclusion concerning this verse: The author of Hebrews said that it was hard to explain the high priestly ministry of Jesus because he felt they weren't listening, they had "become dull of hearing." The Greek word for "dull of hearing" used here is *nothros*. It is found just one other time in the Bible, in Hebrews 6:12 where it is translated "sluggish."

In 2008, I started noticing people were getting frustrated with me because I kept asking them to repeat themselves. Finally, it came to a head when I was in a staff meeting and those around the table lovingly asked me if I was going to get hearing aids. My family agreed; so I had my hearing checked. Sure enough, I needed hearing aids. The first time I put them in my ears I was absolutely amazed! Everything was so crisp and clear. I had no control over my hearing loss—well, almost no control. I did go to rock concerts when I was younger, and I did work for three years in a factory where huge metal presses stamped out metal parts. Yet for the most part my hearing loss is genetic. When it comes to listening concerning spiritual things, many Christians suffer from *hearing loss*. More accurately, Christians suffer from *selective* hearing loss. Often we hear what we want to hear and tune out what we don't want to hear. That is why the author said what he said.

---

[36] O'Brien, *Letter to the Hebrews*, 205fn98.

[37] NIV-New International Version, ESV-English Standard Version, NLT-New Living Translation, RSV-Revised Standard Version.

[38] Lane, *Hebrews 1–8*, 47A, S. 135.

Concerning him we have much to say, and it is hard to explain, since you have become dull of hearing. (Hebrews 5:11)

"You have become" implies that at one point they were *all ears*. They were listening well, learning well, but over time they must have gotten complacent, comfortable; they were not taking in the teaching anymore. They had selected to lose their hearing. Like a gutter on a house in the fall, they had become clogged in their growth and the flowing water of the truth of God's Word had stopped. They had become *nothros*, sluggish, or dull of hearing.

To stop a person from ever becoming a Christian is the first work of Satan. But if he fails in this, he makes it his aim to get believers to become satisfied with where they are so they stop growing in their Christianity. This is a deceptive dilemma that many Christians fall prey to. People stop listening and stop learning. That goes contrary to God's will for us! We have to continue to grow. To do this, we must keep our ears in tune, listening well.

Also, to mature in our Christianity, all of us have to be teachers of the Word of God. That may cause you to say, "Whoa! That can't be right! I'm not gifted in teaching," or, "That's not my gift." The Great Commission (quoted at the beginning of this chapter) says that in order to make disciples we must be *teaching* others to observe God's Word. The author of Hebrews put it this way:

For though by this time you ought to be teachers... (Hebrews 5:12a)

He did not qualify this, or say, "You who have the gift of teaching ought to be teachers." He said, "For though by this time you [*all of you*] ought to be teachers." You may ask, "How can I? I'm not qualified." Some Christians come out of a background where it is sacrilege to even think that they would teach the Bible. Many think, *That should be left to the professionals. I never could nor should assume that role.* The answer, though, is: yes, you can, and you must if you're going to mature as a Christian.

Teachers of the Bible come in all shapes and sizes. When we think of Bible teachers, our minds may quickly go to seminary or Bible college professors, or preachers. We may think of Sunday school teachers, youth group leaders, or pastors. We may even remember a Christian who helped us grow in our faith who is neither a pastor nor a teacher, but that person was definitely gifted. Yet husbands are called to teach their wives (Ephesians 5:22–27); wives and husbands are to partner around the truths of God (e.g., Priscilla and Aquila with Apollos in Acts 18:24–26); parents and grandparents are to instruct their children (e.g., the grandmother and mother of Timothy in 2 Timothy 1:5). Teaching was a common practice among the Israelites.

> Hear, O Israel! The LORD is our God, the LORD is one! You shall love the LORD your God with all your heart and with all your soul and with all your might. These words, which I am commanding you today, shall be on your heart. You shall teach them diligently to your sons and shall talk of them when you sit in your house and when you walk by the way and when you lie down and when you rise up. (Deuteronomy 6:4–7)

So how do we become good teachers? In order to teach, we have to be lifelong learners. There is an old expression that I believe is true: "People like drinking from a running stream rather than a stagnant pool." This means we keep the flow of learning coming in to keep the flow of teaching going out.

> For though by this time you ought to be teachers, you have need again for someone to teach you the elementary principles of the oracles of God, and you have come to need milk and not solid food. (Hebrews 5:12)

As we learned earlier, the book of Hebrews is dated around AD 60. The recipients of this letter (probably a sermon in written form) were not Christians for very long. Yet the author said they should be teaching by now. What can we expect to be a good length of time for someone to become a teacher after becoming a Christian? How can we get people to own the responsibility to teach or to have the confidence to speak the truth into the lives of others, guiding them toward Jesus through the Word of God? How can we get people to be confident enough in God's Word so that they can teach others? These were the issues that the author of Hebrews raised.

> For everyone who partakes only of milk is not accustomed to the word of righteousness, for he is an infant. (Hebrews 5:13)

"Not accustomed to" is one Greek word, *apeiros*, and it is found only here in the whole Bible. It means "lacking knowledge of," or "unacquainted with." To understand this word better, it is helpful to look at the root word: *peira*, which means "an effort to accomplish something," "an effort put forth," "an experiment," or "an experience won by attempting something." Putting the *a* before *peira* (*a-peiros*) makes the word mean the opposite. Therefore, *apeiros* means "not putting forth the effort," "not attempting something." A plague for many Christians is that they won't work at getting to know "the word of righteousness"—the truth of the Bible. The result is they stay as infants, only partaking of milk.

In order to grow up and teach well, we need to practice.

> But solid food is for the mature, who because of practice have their senses trained to discern good and evil. (Hebrews 5:14)

"Practice" means to do something over and over again. I live in Wisconsin. My wife graduated from the University of Wisconsin–Madison, which is also where my son is currently attending school. Therefore, by default, I am a Wisconsin Badger fan. The Badger basketball team this year is doing quite well. One amazing statistic for them is their free-throw shooting percentage. The whole team combined is shooting well over 80 percent. Getting that good doesn't just happen; they spend hours and hours shooting free throws. I have heard that if a player misses a free throw during practice, he has to go over to the head coach, Bo Ryan, ask for forgiveness, and then do push-ups. It's all in fun, yet it is done to push the players to become better at playing basketball. Teaching is no different: You don't become a good teacher by just stepping up to the line and throwing stuff out there. Churches need to create environments where Christians can practice, where it's fun, where we can attempt and experience handling the word of righteousness. Because, remember, as we said earlier, the best way to mature is to teach. When we take on the responsibility to rightly handle the Bible and teach others, we will mature.

Up to this point the text has taught us how to mature. Hebrews 5:14 has already begun to tell us what a mature Christian looks like: He or she is one who discerns good from evil. There are a lot of opinions out there as to what is good and what is evil, or what is right from wrong.

But the only way to know the absolute truth is to go to the Bible. As a Christian continues to learn from the Bible he or she will live what it teaches.

When we grow in our knowledge and understanding of the Bible, we begin to mature as companions with Christ beyond just the basics. The author of Hebrews explained the basics of Christianity using three descriptive pairs. The first pair is "of repentance from dead works and of faith toward God."

> Therefore leaving the elementary teaching about the Christ, let us press on to maturity, not laying again a foundation of repentance from dead works and of faith toward God, (Hebrews 6:1)

"Dead works" is another way of saying "religion." We were in an elders meeting when one of our elders shared that he grew up in "religion." I thought he had a good definition of what it means to practice religion. He said, "What I was doing, I was just doing." In other words, *I went to church, I took communion, I listened to sermons, I did this and I did that*: dead works! What the author of Hebrews was saying is we need to move from that to a life "of faith toward God," where we throw our lives into the Lord's hands, trusting in Him and following Him.

The second descriptive pair is seen at the beginning of the next verse:

> of instruction about washings and laying on of hands, (Hebrews 6:2a)

This is not speaking about New Testament baptisms or the laying on of hands in New Testament times (Matthew 19:15; Acts 8:17–18; 9:17; 1 Timothy 4:14, to name a few). The author was again speaking from the realm of the Old Testament. The instructions were taught from ordinances found in the Old Testament; they were practices that reflected personal purity ("washings") and empowerment from on high ("laying on of hands"). Today, God calls us to holiness that we do not have to accomplish through "washings." And God empowers us to live it through His Spirit working in us. We don't have to receive the Spirit through the laying on of hands like they did in the Old Testament.

The third descriptive pair is found at the end of Hebrews 6:2:

> and the resurrection of the dead and eternal judgment. (Hebrews 6:2b)

The Old Testament doesn't say much about the resurrection or about eternal judgment. Yet when we get to Hebrews 11, we will see that the Old Testament saints looked forward to both of them.

All three of those pairs are the foundation upon which all godly living throughout the ages has been built: *(1) stop the dead works and trust God, (2) be holy as He is holy, and (3) look forward to our resurrection where we will be with God forever.* Yet they describe only the foundation, only the beginning, only the basics of Christianity. It is God's desire that we mature past that, growing in our relationship with Jesus as our high priest (Hebrews 4:15–5:10), understanding God's Sabbath rest (Hebrews 4), learning and developing what it means to have a healthy community or church family (Hebrews 3:12–13), really hearing the voice of God and not hardening our hearts (Hebrews 3), and growing in what it means to be a companion of Christ now and forever (the overarching theme of the book of Hebrews). This is what it means to be mature—*going beyond the basics.*

And mature Christians depend on God.

And this we will do, if God permits. (Hebrews 6:3)

Is there some possibility that God would not permit a Christian to press on toward maturity? I don't think the author just sort of tacked this on—he meant it. This verse is a transitional verse for what will be addressed in the next section. For now, one thing is clear from this verse: we need God. The more I live, the more I know this to be true. We all must know that if we are going to mature as Christians, we need Jesus. We know the struggles, we know the battles, we know that if we are to stay in the game we need to cling to the Lord.

Maturity as a Christian doesn't just happen. It's not like you and I arrive at a certain point with no effort (like a boy all of a sudden starting to grow whiskers). We don't mark our maturity by throwing a party and maybe wearing a toga and getting some gifts. Maturity isn't marked by a specific day that arrives and then, all of a sudden, we're supposed to act like an adult. Maturity as a Christian is a process: we arrive at it (as this text says) and yet we never fully arrive at it. It is a process of listening, learning, teaching, and depending. And all the while, with the Lord's help, we keep growing and growing.

Chapter Eight

GREAT EXPECTATIONS

Hebrews 6:4–9

For eight years I was a pastor of a church in Watseka, Illinois. Watseka is the county seat of Iroquois County, known as one of the most productive corn and soybean growers in the world. Around spring each year the farmers start getting antsy. They are like race horses waiting in the starting gates, raring to go. They have their huge tractors all revved up, their discs for turning over the soil all cleaned up, their planters all fixed up, their seed all bought up, and their sprayers for controlling the weeds all filled up. Imagine if those farmers were halfhearted about getting out in their fields for planting. If they didn't work the soil, if their planters were not planting correctly, if they didn't work to prevent weeds—what then could they expect? A bad harvest? If any one of us had an influence over those farmers who were not giving it their all, wouldn't we want to warn them that their halfheartedness would have bad results?

As we have been going through the book of Hebrews, the author of the book has been warning the Jewish Christians that halfheartedness in their Christian life would have bad results:

> For this reason we must pay much closer attention to what we have heard, so that we do not drift away from it. (Hebrews 2:1)

> How will we escape if we neglect so great a salvation? (Hebrews 2:3a)

Therefore, just as the Holy Spirit says, "Today if you hear His voice, do not harden your hearts." (Hebrews 3:7–8a)

Take care, brethren, that there not be in any one of you an evil, unbelieving heart that falls away from the living God. But encourage one another day after day, as long as it is still called "Today," so that none of you will be hardened by the deceitfulness of sin. (Hebrews 3:12–13)

Therefore, let us fear if, while a promise remains of entering His rest, any one of you may seem to have come short of it. (Hebrews 4:1)

Therefore let us be diligent to enter that rest, so that no one will fall, through following the same example of disobedience. (Hebrews 4:11)

Concerning him we have much to say, and it is hard to explain, since you have become dull of hearing. (Hebrews 5:11)

What would happen if Christians didn't listen? What if Christians did drift away, or fell away, or were being deceived? Hebrews 5–6 is about maturing in our Christianity, but what if the opposite took place and not only did Christians not mature but they fell away from the faith and turned their backs on Christianity and on Christ? It seems evident, according to the verses listed above, as though true Christians can actually do that.

All the warnings throughout the book of Hebrews are addressed to Christians, and all of them are real: Christians can fall away from their Christianity. As we move into this next section, the author of the book of Hebrews starts by reiterating this fact.

For in the case of those who have once been enlightened and have tasted of the heavenly gift and have been made partakers of the Holy Spirit, and have tasted the good word of God and the powers of the age to come, and then have fallen away... (Hebrews 6:4–6a)

Some have said that the author was talking about those who were not true Christians; they may have talked the talk and even walked the walk at one time, but they were never actually saved. The way they describe them goes something like this: "They had faith, but it was not *genuine* faith." However, it appears as though the author intended to go to great lengths to clearly spell out that the people he was describing here were definitely Christians:

1. In their hearts they knew the truth—"those who have once been enlightened."

2. They took the gift from heaven into themselves—"and have tasted of the heavenly gift."

3. They had been partakers (Greek: *metochoi*), partners, companions of the Holy Spirit—"and have been made partakers of the Holy Spirit."

4. They received and enjoyed the good word of God—"and have tasted the good word of God."

5. And they had trusted in—"the powers of the age to come."

If this is not a description of a true born-again believer, then language means nothing and we cannot understand anything in the Bible.[39] In addition to all the warnings that we listed above implying that Christians can fall away, the author was straightforward as he implied that at least some did. Like the soil of a field that has not been properly cared for, the soil of their hearts became hardened against Jesus and was not producing a good harvest:

and then have fallen away, it is impossible to renew them again to repentance, since they again crucify to themselves the Son of God and put Him to open shame. (Hebrews 6:6)

When it says that "it is impossible," it is impossible for whom? Nothing is impossible for God.

Is anything too difficult for the LORD? At the appointed time I will return to you, at this time next year, and Sarah will have a son. (Genesis 18:14)

Ah Lord GOD! Behold, You have made the heavens and the earth by Your great power and by Your outstretched arm! Nothing is too difficult for You. (Jeremiah 32:17)

---

[39] De Haan, *Hebrews*, 104.

And looking at them Jesus said to them, "With people this is impossible, but with God all things are possible." (Matthew 19:26)

For nothing will be impossible with God. (Luke 1:37)

The description given in Hebrews 6:6 is that of a hardened heart against Jesus (remember Hebrews 3:13: "But encourage one another day after day, as long as it is still called 'Today,' so that none of you will be hardened by the deceitfulness of sin"). The word "impossible" used here in verse 6 in the New American Standard Bible is actually placed as the first word in the sentence in the original language, Greek. The sentence began up in Hebrews 6:4. It was put in that prominent position probably to address what the Christians were dealing with: They were having a hard time trying to influence Christians who were turning their backs on Jesus. They found it, in some cases, impossible to turn them back to Him. The author of Hebrews validated their experience by saying, "It is impossible."

I love to go tent camping. This means that I will either get in a canoe or put on my backpack and head off into the woods on some trail and find a place to set up a tent away from the crowds. When setting up a tent, I have to look for three things: (1) I check to make sure there are no dead branches overhead. Otherwise, if a strong wind were to come up overnight and break off that branch, it could fall on top of me. (2) I look for a flat surface. I don't want to set up my tent on the side of the hill. So I try to find a relatively level place without many roots or rocks protruding up from the ground. (3) I make sure that I can push my tent stakes into the ground. It can be quite frustrating getting everything set up (no dead branches above, a nice level surface), the tent laid out on the ground, and then trying to push a stake in the earth only to have it go in a half an inch and hit something hard. I'll poke around trying get around whatever object is under the surface but to no avail. On the surface the ground may look fine, but just underneath it is too hard and I cannot drive any stakes into it.

When Christians turn their backs on Jesus, when they have fallen away from Him and neglected their great salvation, no matter how determined we are to break through the soil of their hearts, it is like trying to drive a stake through a rock—"it is impossible."

Notice what it is impossible to do:

and then have fallen away, it is impossible to renew them again to repentance, since they again crucify to themselves the Son of God and put Him to open shame. (Hebrews 6:6)

The author says, "It is impossible to renew them again to repentance." The word "repentance" means to change the mind. And in this context it means to change the mind concerning their hardened hearts. It does not say, "It is impossible to renew them again to *salvation.*" "The writer of Hebrews 6 is not talking about losing salvation.... What a gloomy gospel it would be—telling people in this day of grace that it is impossible for them to be saved."[40]

It is impossible to have them change their minds about how they are thinking and acting. It is impossible because they have the same heart toward Jesus as those who crucified Him: They want to be done with Him and to get rid of Him, so they "put Him to open shame." Some translations say "treat Him with contempt." In other words, these Christians are treating Jesus as worthless or even as vile. These are strong words from Hebrews.

I know Christians personally who have this kind of hardened heart. I have tried to bring up the subject of Jesus and they just shut it down. I've often wondered why they've turned their backs on Him, and when I ask, there is an immediate flare-up of anger, accusation, and attack. I don't like going there and talking about it because it seems so volatile. I think, *Can't we just have a rational, reasonable adult conversation?* But I know the answer I will get: "No!" They will say something like, "You are so judgmental," and honestly, I will not even really have said anything. It's as if the tent stake just bends because their heart has become hardened. And you can hear it in their voice: "*I don't want anything to do with Jesus.*" It's like He's become vile to them.

I would imagine that I am not alone in my experience with Christians who have fallen away from the faith. You probably have experienced this too. I have known people who were in leadership in ministry but turned their backs on Jesus. I even had a seminary professor (with all that schooling and all those years) who fell away and is no longer serving in ministry. Here is a sobering fact: according

---

[40] De Haan, *Hebrews*, 98–99.

to all the warnings, and this passage in particular, it can happen to any of us. Here's why: Christians don't let the soil of their hearts continue to be cultivated.

> For ground that drinks the rain which often falls on it and brings forth vegetation useful to those for whose sake it is also tilled, receives a blessing from God; but if it yields thorns and thistles, it is worthless and close to being cursed, and it ends up being burned. (Hebrews 6:7–8)

Do you see the contrast in the productivity of the soils here? What makes the difference? The only way that the ground produces thorns and thistles is if it is not tilled, not cultivated, not weeded. If the ground doesn't have a consistent working over it, its productivity goes downhill fast.

To avoid the slow drift (Hebrews 2:1), the hardening of our hearts (Hebrews 3:7–8), the deceitfulness of sin (Hebrews 3:12–13), we have to let God turn over the soil of our hearts on a consistent basis—regularly. The way that it is done is by drinking in the rain of His Word. By letting it fall on us often through personal Bible reading, listening to the preaching of the Word, and being in fellowship with other Christians who we allow to speak God's truth into our lives. At times, this may feel like we are being tilled open, turned over, and laid bare. But we must be humble and allow our lives to be worked in such a way that we will bring forth vegetation that is useful for others. According to the end of verse 7, if we allow ourselves to be cultivated and used by God for the benefit of others, we will experience the blessing of God.

> For ground that drinks the rain which often falls on it and brings forth vegetation useful to those for whose sake it is also tilled, receives a blessing from God; (Hebrews 6:7)

If some people do fall away and are so hardened that they won't listen, what are the consequences? Some think, *God is so loving and good and forgiving that he will just let it go.* Actually, God won't just let it go. If we don't let our hearts get cultivated, God will, sooner or later, break them up like a farmer breaks up hardened soil.

> but if it yields thorns and thistles, it is worthless and close to being cursed, and it ends up being burned. (Hebrews 6:8)

When we see words like "cursed" and "burned," our minds might quickly jump to the concept of being sent to hell. Actually, "cursed" is used in a variety of ways throughout the Bible, all meaning that there is some bad stuff coming or has already come. It does not always mean "hell" (James 3:10; 2 Peter 2:14). And to be "burned,"— unless there is a modifier like "eternal" or "unquenchable" or it is not speaking literally about something burning (like the burning bush in Exodus 3:2)—is a picture of God's judgment or discipline.[41] What Hebrews 6:8 is saying is that either the Lord will discipline a hardened Christian or a time will come when he or she will be judged. A hardened Christian will not be cast into hell, but there will be a harsh reprimand for living a useless or worthless life (Hebrews 6:8). The author of Hebrews pulls no punches when he references this later on in the book:

> For we know Him who said, "Vengeance is Mine, I will repay." And again, "The Lord will judge His people." It is a terrifying thing to fall into the hands of the living God. (Hebrews 10:30–31)

This is serious stuff. For those who don't see God this way, C. S. Lewis may capture your picture of who God is:

We want, in fact, not so much a father in Heaven as a grandfather in Heaven—a senile benevolence who, as they say, "likes to see young people enjoying themselves," and whose plan for the universe was simply that it might be truly said at the end of each day, "a good time was had by all."[42]

No, this is not how the Bible describes God. God is a loving Father who will not wink at our hard hearts. He will not let us get away with that kind of behavior, and He will correct us either in this life with discipline (Hebrews 12:4–11) or in the next when we stand before His judgment seat (1 Corinthians 3:10–15; 2 Corinthians 5:10). But He does not cast Christians into hell.

The author of Hebrews was a pastor at heart. So with the gentle words of a shepherd he concluded this section with these words:

---

[41] Wilkin, *Confident in Christ*, 155.

[42] Lewis, *Problem of Pain*, 35.

But, beloved, we are convinced of better things concerning you, and things that accompany salvation, though we are speaking in this way. (Hebrews 6:9)

As he had done throughout the book, the author of Hebrews gave encouraging words to his audience.

There was a young pastor who started at a church in a rural town. He wanted to get to know the people of his congregation, and so he went out one spring to meet one of the farmers. The crop had just come up, and the farmer was out spraying his field. The pastor waited at the end of the field until the farmer came near. When the farmer shut down the tractor and got out of it, he walked over to the pastor. The pastor said, "This is some fine land God has given to you." The farmer replied, "Amen, pastor! But, honestly, you should have seen this field when God had it all to Himself; I had to do a lot of work to get it to where it's at today."[43]

Just as God could, of course, maintain a field and grow bumper crops of corn, soybeans, or any other produce, He could maintain our faith and relationship with Him without any help on our part. However, God has chosen to give us a vital role to play. In order not to fall away, we have to open the soil of our hearts and drink in the rain of God's Word and allow others to cultivate us—to speak into our lives. And when we do, we will bear vegetation that is useful for others and we will experience the blessings of our Lord.

---

[43] Wilkin, *Confident in Christ*, 157.

CHAPTER NINE

SATISFACTION

Hebrews 6:10–20

In our Declaration of Independence, it is declared that a God-given right people have, along with life and liberty, is the opportunity to pursue happiness. For most people their whole lives are never-ending pursuits to try to be happy, or content. When life is difficult, it is not uncommon for people to say, *"I just want to be happy,"* or, *"I deserve to be happy."* There are many pursuits of happiness we go after because each of us has a deep desire for satisfaction. We lose some weight thinking others will notice and we will feel good. But to maintain the good feelings, we find we need to do more to get in even *better* shape. We pursue happiness by entering into a new relationship—we feel so good, so excited, so filled up. Advertisers prey on this desire of ours: Get the latest technology, or fashion, or the all new design of the latest luxury car; and we think if we buy these things they will bring satisfaction or happiness. But it doesn't take long until what was new and exciting becomes routine, mundane, and familiar. And our happiness begins to fade.

God desires for us to mature in our relationship with Him. One of the signs of maturing as Christians is a consistent sense of satisfaction. I'm not talking about a season of satisfaction, or a feeling that is here today and fades tomorrow like most people experience when something new or exciting comes into their lives. We can tell we are maturing as Christians when we experience a deep, steady satisfaction that does not waver over the years.

God wants us to know and experience His satisfaction now. And, not only right now, but He wants us to know it consistently forever: No more experimenting; no more hoping against hope to find and maintain happiness. A satisfaction, right now, that does not wane, that does not falter or fail us. It is natural for us to search for things to satisfy us—God made us that way. I agree with our Declaration of Independence—it is a God-given gift. He made us to be searchers for satisfaction. He made us to take some ownership of our own joy or contentment. God did not make us to be bystanders, as if we sit back like a bump-on-a-log and somehow, miraculously, we know satisfaction in our lives. God did not design us so that He does all the work and all of a sudden, through no effort of our own, we experience that satisfaction we're looking for. No, God knows how we can contribute to our own satisfaction.

The Bible is clear that the way we experience satisfaction is to live for what we were made for. In Matthew 22:34–40, Christ was explicit when He responded to a Pharisee's question: "Teacher, which is the greatest commandment in the Law?" Jesus replied, "'Love the Lord your God with all your heart and with all your soul and with all your mind.' This is the first and greatest commandment. And the second is like it: 'Love your neighbor as yourself.' All the Law and the Prophets hang on these two commandments" (NIV). As we move into our next section of the book of Hebrews, it begins by saying,

> For God is not unjust so as to forget your work and the love which you have shown toward His name, in having ministered and in still ministering to the saints. (Hebrews 6:10)

This verse says that the way we show our love for God is through being actively involved in ministry. And did you see who we are supposed to be ministering to? *The saints!* Building up Christians, helping them grow in the Lord, brings satisfaction into our lives. And aren't Christians included in the second half of the Great Commandment, "Love your neighbor as yourself" (Matthew 22:39)? First, we are to love God, then love others. It's as if the two go hand in hand: We can't say "I love God" without loving others. And we can't say "I love my neighbor" without investing our time and energy into ministering to them.

The whole theme of the book of Hebrews is about being companions with Christ. You and I cannot grow as companions with Christ unless we are growing as Christians. We cannot grow as Christians unless others are investing in us and we in them. So to love God and mature in Christ, we must move our attention away from ourselves, which is what a loving heart does, and get involved in ministry. By serving others, we help them grow in their understanding and relationship with Christ. This is the only way to find satisfaction that lasts.

We can't be involved in ministry just by association either. Like saying, "We're doing some great stuff at our church: children's ministry is booming, youth group is great, people are getting saved and growing in the Lord," and the reality is we're not helping out. God's design for the church is that we work together as Christians. Which means each of us, as individuals, must take responsibility; each of us must be invested; each of us must be involved. Look at how the author of Hebrews put it in the next verse:

And we desire that each one of you show the same diligence so as to realize the full assurance of hope until the end... (Hebrews 6:11)

"We desire that each one of you"—each of us—takes ownership to "show the same diligence." Why? "To realize the full assurance of hope until the end." In other words, to feel satisfaction for years and years—*until the end*—forever! Investing our hearts and souls into ministry is truly a satisfying labor of love.

And we desire that each one of you show the same diligence so as to realize the full assurance of hope until the end, so that you will not be sluggish, but imitators of those who through faith and patience inherit the promises. (Hebrews 6:11–12)

Another reason that is given for showing this kind of intensity in serving in ministry is so that we don't become "sluggish." This word means to be lazy or dull; it is the opposite of working hard, or being diligent. We came across this word, "sluggish," earlier in this letter (the only other time this word is found in the Bible). It was used in

Hebrews 5:11 where the author said the Christians receiving this letter had become *dull* of hearing.

In Hebrews, God issues a call to get on His team, to be diligent in serving Him through ministry. Because it is through being on God's team that God offers true satisfaction. He actually promises it. Did you see that in verse 12?

> so that you will not be sluggish, but imitators of those who through faith and patience inherit the promises. (Hebrews 6:12)

The word "inherit" is a verb in the present tense and an active participle, meaning it is a continuous action in the present. This is important to note because many people can read this verse and assume that the "promises" are something that come in the future (after we die). However, God wants us to know His involvement in our lives—His promises—in a continuous way, right now. The author painted a picture of experiencing God's promises through a patriarch, an ancient icon of the Bible: Abraham.

> For when God made the promise to Abraham, since He could swear by no one greater, He swore by Himself, saying, "I will surely bless you and I will surely multiply you." And so, having patiently waited, he obtained the promise. (Hebrews 6:13–15)

Do you remember what happened with Abraham? Let me give you a quick overview of his adult life:

- Age 75: Abraham received the promise (Genesis 12:1–4).

- Age 86: Abraham received the oath/covenant (Genesis 15:17–21).

- Age 99: Abraham received another confirmation of the oath, and God instituted circumcision (Genesis 17:1–27).

- Age 100: Abraham and Sarah had Isaac (Genesis 21:1–5).

- Age 137: Abraham's wife, Sarah, died (Genesis 23:1–2).

- Age 140: Abraham's son Isaac married Rebekah (Genesis 24:67). They had trouble getting pregnant, but then Rebekah was expecting twins (Genesis 25:20–24).

- Age 160: Abraham saw his grandsons Esau and Jacob come into this world (Genesis 21:1-5; 25:25-26).

- Age 175: Abraham died "an old man and satisfied with life" (Genesis 25:7–8).

The first seventy-five years of his life, Abraham was not following the one true God, and I would imagine he experienced discontentment. But the last one hundred years, the Lord brought to his life true satisfaction! As with Abraham, God has given to us a promise and an oath.

> For men swear by one greater than themselves, and with them an oath given as confirmation is an end of every dispute. In the same way God, desiring even more to show to the heirs of the promise the unchangeableness of His purpose, interposed with an oath, so that by two unchangeable things in which it is impossible for God to lie, we who have taken refuge would have strong encouragement to take hold of the hope set before us. (Hebrews 6:16–18)

An oath in the first century was a big deal. Once a person swore with an oath, nothing more needed to be said. It sealed the deal; it was a binding confirmation (Matthew 5:33; 14:6–9; 26:69–74; Luke 1:67–77; Acts 2:30; Hebrews 6:16; James 5:12). The hope that is set before us is the blessings we can share, which Abraham experienced. The "two unchangeable things" that were blessings to Abraham and are blessings to us are (1) God's promises, which He always keeps and (2) an eternity with the Lord (Genesis 12:1–4). We experience these "two unchangeable things" through the promise of forgiveness and eternal life (John 10:10; 17:3). The oath was sealed through the blood covenant made by the death of His Son, Jesus. God gave us a real and unchangeable hope.

> so that by two unchangeable things in which it is impossible for God to lie, we who have taken refuge would have strong encouragement to take hold of the hope set before us. (Hebrews 6:18)

Can you see the implication here? The author wrote, "We who have taken refuge," which implies not every Christian takes refuge in the Lord. We have already seen that this is true (Hebrews 6:1–9). Some Christians produce thorns and thistles for the Lord—they turn their backs on Him with hardened hearts. Some Christians don't take refuge; they are the ones who don't know God's *strong encouragement* (as the verse above says)—His satisfaction.

One afternoon in the dead of winter, my wife, daughters, and I had pulled into our driveway and were going to park the van in the garage when I noticed what at first glance seemed to be a brown chunk of ice in the middle of the garage—the kind that sticks to your car after building up behind the tires. Those of us who live in the northern sections of our country know what I'm talking about. However, as we drove closer, I could see that it wasn't a chunk of ice; it was a bird, a big bird (not to be confused with Big Bird on *Sesame Street*). I found out later it was a Cooper's hawk. If you do a Google search for images of this animal, you will see that it is a beautiful creature. I stopped the van in the driveway, not pulling it into the garage, and I warned my family not to go close. We left the garage door open, but the hawk would not leave. That was on a Friday. All day Saturday, we left the garage door open, and it still would not fly out. As I looked closer, I could see that one of its wings looked injured. So, Saturday night, we thawed out some ground venison meat and put it out in the garage. By Sunday morning the venison was gone. We decided that we would keep the hawk in the garage and call whoever we needed to on Monday to help this injured animal. We got a hold of an animal rescue team who came out, captured the hawk, and confirmed to us what kind it was and what its injuries were.

That poor animal was stuck in our garage for three days. God made the Cooper's hawk to soar, not to hang out in a garage; but it was not able to because of its wounds. God made people to soar, but so many people don't. It's like they are stuck, wounded, trapped. God made us to know His satisfaction, but so many people (Christians even) don't know it. However, unlike that Cooper's hawk, most people are stuck because they choose to be stuck. If we're not soaring, it's because we haven't taken refuge in our relationship with the Lord.

God wants all of His adopted children (which is what Christians are: John 1:12; Romans 8:15; Ephesians 1:5) to live in satisfaction, where it defines our lives. He wants us to soar in Him. He doesn't want our experience of knowing His joy to be the exception, but the rule—where it isn't for the select few, but for all Christians—to live lives of satisfaction.

> This hope we have as an anchor of the soul, a hope both sure and steadfast… (Hebrews 6:19a)

I love that imagery of an *anchor*—"hope" holds us steady. There was a school system in a large city that had a positive program to help children keep up their schoolwork if they were in the hospital for a while. A teacher who was assigned to the program received a routine phone call asking her to visit a child at the children's hospital. She took his name and room number and talked briefly with the child's regular class teacher. His classroom teacher said, "We're studying nouns and adverbs in his class now, and I'd be grateful if you could help him understand them so he doesn't fall too far behind." The teacher who worked in the hospital went to the area of the hospital where the boy was, and instantly she knew it could be bad. As she made her way to his room, she found herself in the burn unit of the hospital. When she entered the room, she could see that the boy was badly burned and in great pain. She tried to keep her composure and said, "I've been sent by your school to help you with nouns and adverbs." She worked hard to help him, even though he was so badly burned and couldn't talk.

The next day, as the teacher was coming back to work with the boy some more, a nurse stopped her in the hall and asked her, "What did you do to that boy?" The teacher felt like she must have done something wrong and began to apologize. But the nurse said, "No. You don't understand. He is fighting back; he's responding to the treatment. It's as though he's decided to live." Two weeks later the boy could finally talk, and he explained he had given up hope until that teacher arrived. He said, "They wouldn't send a teacher to work on nouns and adverbs with a boy who's dyin', would they?"[44]

Hope is an anchor for the soul; it's what breathes life into us. It is *the* ingredient that God gives to ground us, to stabilize us, to enable us to experience His satisfaction.

A key part of the hope that we have is we can experience entering

---

[44] Lenehan, *Best of Bits & Pieces*, 93–94.

God's throne room. Which means we can draw near to God at any time; we can know Him; we can know that He will guide us and that we can love Him and He loves us; we can know that we have an eternity to look forward to with Him!

> This hope we have as an anchor of the soul, a hope both sure and steadfast *and one which enters within the veil,* (Hebrews 6:19)

The "veil" was that thick curtain that separated the holy of holies from the rest of the Jewish tabernacle or the temple. The veil was what separated the place of worship from the inner room where God dwelled with His people. What Hebrews 6:19 and then into verse 20 is saying is we have a hope, anchored in Jesus. And because of Jesus, you and I as Christians can come before God at any time. We can because of the ministry of Jesus, which He is doing right now, on our behalf.

> where Jesus has entered as a forerunner for us, having become a high priest forever according to the order of Melchizedek. (Hebrews 6:20)

We can know the high priestly ministry of Jesus right now in our lives. How? He has torn the divider between us and God as our Father. The veil was torn when Jesus died for us (Matthew 27:51; Mark 15:38; Luke 23:45). We can now enter the holy of holies; we can unite with the Lord and know His compassion and His care. We can grow in our relationship with Him to the point where we know what makes His heart beat faster with joy or what causes Him to be sad or angry. We can know He is using us to do ministry. In all of this, we can know we're walking side by side with Him as His companions—where we know at our core we are partnering with Him—and in that there is genuine satisfaction!

PART III

JESUS, OUR HIGH PRIEST

Hebrews 7:1–10:25

CHAPTER TEN

A PICTURE IS WORTH
A THOUSAND WORDS

Hebrews 7:1–10

The title of this chapter is an expression you may have heard before. I was doing a little searching on the Internet as to that expression's origin: it appears to have its beginnings in China. There is a Chinese proverb that says, "One picture is worth ten thousand words." And, as it emerged in the United States in the 1920s, the number was reduced from ten thousand to one thousand.[45] Communicators—those who do public speaking, write books, teach, are on the radio, etc.—like to turn that phrase around because they use words to paint pictures. One of the main skills you have to learn, hone, and develop if you're going to communicate well is to create pictures with words.

As we have been going through our study, the author of Hebrews has been hinting at the ministry Jesus has as our high priest. And I get the impression, as he interacted with the Jewish Christians who were the recipients of this letter, that he could tell they did not understand what he was trying to communicate to them. I would imagine the people then (like people today) were saying, "What does it mean that

---

[45] "A Picture Is Worth a Thousand Words," accessed January 18, 2014, www.phrases.org.uk/meanings/a-picture-is-worth-a-thousand-words.html.

Jesus is our high priest? What does it look like?" So the author decided to create a picture out of words to help his audience understand the ministry Jesus had in their lives.

In the last chapter the author concluded that Jesus had "become a high priest forever according to the order of Melchizedek" (Hebrews 6:20). As we begin to understand Hebrews 7, we will see the author explaining Jesus's high priestly ministry through painting a picture of Melchizedek. However, in so doing this, his main goal was to paint a picture of Jesus. In other words, the author used Melchizedek to illustrate the ministry of Jesus.

The first brushstroke in this painting is seen in Hebrews 7:1:

> For this Melchizedek, king of Salem, priest of the Most High God, who met Abraham as he was returning from the slaughter of the kings and blessed him... (Hebrews 7:1)[46]

Let me share the history behind Hebrews 7:1. Back in the days of Abraham there were many kings. They were not rulers over great empires; they ruled small sections of land and small groups or clans of people. They were more like our mayors today rather than governors or the president.

Yet, like many in positions of power, some of those kings began to form alliances in order to gain more power. There were four kings who formed an alliance in the land between the Tigris and Euphrates Rivers, where Abraham once lived. They first moved west conquering different cities, then they moved south (probably on the same road that Abraham traveled years earlier) to the east of the Sea of Galilee. Traveling along the Jordan River, they continued south and east of the Dead Sea.

Word had gotten out that these kings were coming. So five kings who ruled to the south and west of the Dead Sea became allies to fight the four from the north. The battle was fought on the plains south of the Dead Sea, and the five kings to the south were not strong enough for the four kings from the north. The southern kings and their armies suffered many casualties and ended up fleeing to the hills.

The four kings then headed back north, taking captives—men,

---

[46] What this is referring to is found in Genesis 14.

women, and children—and many possessions along the way. But they made a mistake. They took a man named Lot and his family and possessions from a town called Sodom (of the famed Sodom and Gomorrah). The reason why that was a mistake was because Lot was Abraham's nephew. Abraham found out about it and rounded up 318 of his best trained men to go and rescue Lot and his family. He chased those four kings about 120 miles north to a place called Dan, just north of the Sea of Galilee. He fought and routed those kings even farther north to a place called Hobah, north of Damascus, where he finally defeated the kings and rescued Lot and his family. Not only did he recover all of their possessions but he acquired many more from the battle. While heading south, back to where he lived, Abraham (who at that time was known as Abram) met Melchizedek. Let's read about their interaction:

> Then after his return from the defeat of Chedorlaomer and the kings who were with him, the king of Sodom went out to meet him at the valley of Shaveh (that is, the King's Valley). And Melchizedek king of Salem brought out bread and wine; now he was a priest of God Most High. He blessed him and said, "Blessed be Abram of God Most High, possessor of heaven and earth; and blessed be God Most High, who has delivered your enemies into your hand." He gave him a tenth of all. (Genesis 14:17–20)

That's it. That's the entire painting of Melchizedek in all of the Old Testament. Outside of Psalm 110:4, Melchizedek is not referred to in the Bible again until the book of Hebrews. There he's mentioned in chapters 5, 6, and now in chapter 7. Let's read that first verse of Hebrews 7 again.

> For this Melchizedek, king of Salem, priest of the Most High God, who met Abraham as he was returning from the slaughter of the kings and blessed him, (Hebrews 7:1)

Remember that the author was painting a picture of Jesus. As Melchizedek did with Abraham, Jesus meets us where we are and blesses us. After Abraham fought his enemies, the first thing Melchizedek did was to go out and meet him. And he brought to Abraham wine and bread. Wine and bread are considered comfort food—food that makes the heart glad, that brings warmth to the soul (Psalm 104:15). What Melchizedek did was he tangibly blessed Abraham. Then he confirmed Abraham's relationship with God Most High and reaffirmed to Abraham that God was working in his life. That is the high priestly ministry of Jesus in our lives today: We have our battles (spiritual, emotional, relational, physical) where life can be tough. But Jesus meets us where we are and brings comfort, warmth, and gladness. And He blesses us by confirming our relationship with God and reaffirming that God is still working in our lives.

The author of Hebrews went on to say that, just as Melchizedek was a king back in the days of Abraham, Jesus is our king of righteousness and king of peace today.

> to whom also Abraham apportioned a tenth part of all the spoils, was first of all, by the translation of his name, king of righteousness, and then also king of Salem, which is king of peace. (Hebrews 7:2)

Again, this is a picture being painted of Jesus as our high priest. Like Melchizedek, Jesus is not only a priest, He is also a king. The question for those reading this verse then as well as now is, "Is Jesus my king?" Is He on the throne of our lives? To be subjects of the king, we act on the king's behalf, we live to please the king, and we seek the leadership of the king over our lives. If we let Jesus be king in our lives, He will lead us into righteousness, which means He will guide us into holiness, right living, and godly wisdom. And if we let Jesus be our king, He will lead us into peace: away from fear and anxiety to a place of calm and steadiness.

As illustrated in the account of Melchizedek, Jesus is and always will minister as our high priest.

> Without father, without mother, without genealogy, having neither beginning of days nor end of life, but made like the Son of God, he remains a priest perpetually. (Hebrews 7:3)

Some scholars speculate that Melchizedek was actually Jesus. They say this because of the description in Hebrews 7:3. One thing to notice about this verse is that Melchizedek was "made" like Jesus. It was not Christ who was made similar to Melchizedek, but Melchizedek was made like the Son of God. Melchizedek was made to resemble Jesus, not the other way around.

Melchizedek has been honoured to share in the dignity belonging properly to the Son of God. It is because of this that his history is so narrated in God's record of him that, as far as that record goes, his is presented as without ancestry, birth, or death. Not that he was actually without these, else would he be eternal, uncreated, immortal, the Son of God Himself. This has been suggested, but the thought is forbidden by the statement that Melchizedek was made, and made like unto the Son of God. No one can be made like unto himself, for he is already himself.[47]

No doubt, Melchizedek actually had a beginning; but what was recorded of him paints a picture of Jesus. Being "made like the Son of God" meant that the record of Melchizedek, written about fifteen hundred years earlier, was going to be used to paint a picture of Jesus. The picture that the history of Melchizedek would paint would be that Jesus is eternal.

Therefore, even now we can go to God for help (as we saw in Hebrews 4:15–16). And what we receive from Him now is just a small taste of what eternity will bring when we walk the streets of gold with Him, being with Him in His glory. Then He will continue to minister to us and we will continue to draw near to Him.

The author of Hebrews continued to paint more details about Jesus. His next brushstroke would illustrate the fact that Jesus is greater than the greatest of any Old Testament person. These Jewish Christians all thought Abraham was the top person in the mind of God when he was alive on the earth. Yet look what the author of Hebrews wrote:

> Now observe how great this man was to whom Abraham, the patriarch, gave a tenth of the choicest spoils. (Hebrews 7:4)

Abraham, the patriarch (the man whom God used to establish His plans for eternity and to outline the whole message of the Bible), gave Melchizedek a tenth of his "choicest spoils," which means he gave a tenth off the top, or of the best he had, in order to honor him.

Similarly, many churches today take offerings. The comment that is often said is "This is a form of worship," meaning this is the way of showing Jesus honor; just as Abraham showed Melchizedek honor.

---

[47] Lang, *Epistle to the Hebrews*, 116.

Giving 10 percent off the top—a tithe, like Abraham did, is a tangible picture from us to the Lord in giving Him honor. Giving a tenth must be done freely, not under compulsion. Abraham lived long before the law was given. No one forced him to give 10 percent; he just gave out of the deep desire to honor Melchizedek.

> And those indeed of the sons of Levi who receive the priest's office have commandment in the Law to collect a tenth from the people, that is, from their brethren, although these are descended from Abraham. But the one whose genealogy is not traced from them collected a tenth from Abraham... (Hebrews 7:5–6a)

When the apostle Paul talked about giving, he described the kind of heart we should have:

> Each one must do just as he has purposed in his heart, not grudgingly or under compulsion, for God loves a cheerful giver. (2 Corinthians 9:7)

As Christians, we need to have the heart of Abraham. No one is forced to give 10 percent. It's up to each of us to freely choose what we're going to do, what we're going to give. The concept of giving a tithe was practiced long before the law, and it can still be practiced, even though we are not under the law anymore.

In a small church in the Deep South, a preacher was moving to the end of the sermon with a crescendo. The preacher said, "This church, like a crippled man Jesus healed, has got to get up and walk for Jesus's sake." And a person sitting in the pew yelled out, "That's right, Reverend, let it walk." And there were a few more "Mm-hmms" and "Amens." Then the preacher added, "This church, like Elijah on Mount Carmel, to bring honor to God, has got to run!" And a number of people in the congregation gave a hearty "Run, let it run, Preacher, let it run!" Finally, growing even louder, the preacher belted out, "This church, we have got to mount up on wings like eagles and fly— bringing glory to Jesus!" And the congregation stood to its feet and declared, "Let it fly, Pastor, let it fly!" Then the pastor added, "Now if this church is going to fly for Jesus, it's gonna take a little money to do it." And everyone in the congregation just stood there staring blankly at the preacher. Finally, a voice coming somewhere from the middle of the congregation said somewhat meekly, "Um…walkin's good. I think, let it walk."[48]

We are free to soar for Jesus if we want to, and like Abraham with Melchizedek, we can bring Jesus the honor He deserves through our giving. It was clear that Abraham treated Melchizedek as greater than himself. This was a picture that the author of Hebrews painted for the recipients of Hebrews and for us today: we are to treat Jesus as greater than ourselves.

> But the one whose genealogy is not traced from them collected a tenth from Abraham and blessed the one who had the promises. But without any dispute the lesser is blessed by the greater. (Hebrews 7:6–7)

Do we treat Jesus as greater or lesser than us? If Jesus is treated as less than us, then we will call on Him only in a time of crisis. We will have the mentality that He is there *only* when we need Him. We say in our hearts, "He exists for me," rather than, "I exist for Him." Jesus is lesser than us when we feel, "I and my stuff come before Him and His stuff." Jesus is not greater than us in our minds when we believe, "I am making *my* money, living *my* life, spending *my* time the way I want to. And how Jesus would have me spend those things doesn't really matter." One more sign that Jesus is less than us is when doing things for Him takes priority over relating to and relying on Him. Let me explain: As Christians, some of us can be so busy doing ministry that we don't have time to get to know the One we are doing ministry for. Another way to say it is Jesus is less than us in our lives when our function trumps our faith.

We will know the blessing of the high priestly ministry of Jesus when we draw near to Him in faith and relate to Him through prayer and through His Word. The apostle Peter put it this way:

> Now for this very reason also, applying all diligence, in your faith supply moral excellence, and in your moral excellence, knowledge, and in your knowledge, self-control, and in your self-control, perseverance, and in your perseverance, godliness, and in your godliness, brotherly kindness, and in your brotherly kindness, love. (2 Peter 1:5–7)

---

[48] Adapted from Swindoll, *Tardy Oxcart*, 389–90.

That is what the picture looks like when Jesus is *greater* than us.

The Jewish Christians, the original recipients of the letter of Hebrews, held the Levitical priesthood as the ultimate priesthood. Next, the author of Hebrews illustrated that Jesus, as our high priest, was and is superior to the Levitical priesthood.

> In this case mortal men receive tithes, but in that case one receives them, of whom it is witnessed that he lives on. And, so to speak, through Abraham even Levi, who received tithes, paid tithes, for he was still in the loins of his father when Melchizedek met him. (Hebrews 7:8–10)

Abraham was the great-grandfather of Levi. Since Abraham put himself below Melchizedek, the priesthood of his great-grandson Levi would be considered below the priesthood of Melchizedek as well. As a picture of Jesus, Melchizedek illustrates that Jesus is superior to every human priesthood or office (or anything else for that matter).

Just as the author of Hebrews urged the Jewish Christians to make sure that Jesus was superior in their lives, I wonder, is Jesus superior to everyone else in our lives? It's pretty easy for us to get all worked up about different people in our world. We can get all riled up to defend, to fight, or to support a politician, a pundit, an athlete, or even the pope. And there's really nothing wrong with that. However, do we show even more passion for our high priest, Jesus? Do we defend Him? Do we stand up for Him and His will in our world? Do we fight for His righteousness in the public square? Do we go to battle for Him?

Because we are Christians, Jesus is our high priest. If a picture is worth a thousand words, then Melchizedek is a picture of Jesus. He meets us where we are and brings comfort and gladness to our souls. He is our king who brings peace into our lives when we follow Him. Yet in this painting there is another figure: Abraham, who illustrates someone else. Abraham paints a picture for us to see how we are supposed to treat Jesus. Abraham treated Melchizedek with honor, dignity, and respect, and we must do the same with Jesus.

CHAPTER ELEVEN

PERFECT PATHWAY

Hebrews 7:11–28

There are two different types of people in our world: those who want to connect with God in some way, and those who do not. Even though a great number do not give much thought concerning God, all sorts of people are spiritually minded, believe in a higher state of existence, and think there is a way to get there. They often ponder the possibility of connecting to a higher power, a deity, a god, or at least getting to a place of eternal bliss. It is probable that one of the primary components of their thinking is *What does it take to reach that place of bliss or to be connected to God forever?* or *What does it take for God to accept me?*

For those who believe they have found the right answer, the perfect solution, or the way that works best for them, I wonder: Is there ever any room to challenge their beliefs? Is there any openness to the possibility that what they hold to be *the truth* is actually not complete, or a bit misguided, or even totally wrong? Even we who would consider ourselves to be Christians, are we open to being challenged in what we believe? Are we willing to ask, "Is that right," "Is that really true," "Will I really connect with and be accepted by God through that pathway?"

So what is the pathway to God? Most people would say that it is not *the* pathway to God but the *pathways* to God. It seems logical that

God would allow different ways to get to Him or to be accepted by Him. Their thinking is this: as long as you are devoted and serious about the pathway you choose, God will accept your devotion and commitment and therefore accept you. God would not reject people if they were serious about their beliefs, would He?

The religion closest to Christianity is Judaism. It is the very root from which our faith has come. One of the pathways to God the Jews held to was being made right before God through the priests and participating in the activities of the Jewish temple. They believed the priest performed sacrifices according to the law to make them right before God. As we continue in our study through the book of Hebrews, look at what the author said about that pathway:

> Now if perfection was through the Levitical priesthood (for on the basis of it the people received the Law), what further need was there for another priest to arise according to the order of Melchizedek, and not be designated according to the order of Aaron? (Hebrews 7:11)

Aaron was the brother of Moses. Both of them were descendants of Levi. God established the Levitical priesthood, but it wasn't put in place to make the Hebrew people, the Jews, perfectly acceptable to God. The people would present their offerings of animals or grain, in accordance with the law, to the Levitical priests. The Levites who served in the priesthood would perform sacrifices according to all the regulations of the law. But who they were and what they did would never be the pathway to God no matter how devout the priests were or how dedicated the followers of that path were. There had to be another path. And it was according to the order of Melchizedek (remember, we heard a lot about him in the previous chapter).

If keeping the law by bringing offerings and sacrifices to the Levitical priests is not a legitimate pathway, then what about the hundreds or even thousands of different belief systems or pathways out there? Buddhists say you have to hold to an eightfold pathway to reach nirvana (which is an eternal state of bliss). Islam says you must believe its six doctrines and practice its five pillars in order to earn your salvation. Jehovah's Witnesses and Mormons both teach that you must work for your salvation in order to be found worthy. And the list goes on and on.

Even within what we would consider Christianity there are variances in what we believe is God's plan and path for us to be with Him. Take, for instance, Catholicism: Catholics believe we are made right before God through faith in Jesus. They align with evangelical Christians in teaching that we must believe that through the death, burial, and resurrection of Jesus we can live with Him forever. However, they teach that that is the beginning of our salvation journey. They say we are to build on the foundation of Jesus with good works in order to allow God to infuse His goodness and move us toward being with Him forever. According to Catholicism, the good works we must perform are practicing the seven sacraments in order to merit salvation. They would blend faith in Jesus plus good works.

People have been devoted throughout history to these and many other paths. So who is right? And if the author of Hebrews already indicated that perfection (being made right before God) is not through the Levitical priesthood, then maybe other pathways are wrong.

The Hebrew Christians who first received this letter needed to be corrected in their thinking. Much like the Catholic Church, it appears that these young Christians believed in Jesus but then added good works according to the law as the pathway to God. What the author of Hebrews will clarify in the remaining verses of Hebrews 7 is that *Jesus is the only way*. Nothing more and nothing less.

> For when the priesthood is changed, of necessity there takes place a change of law also. (Hebrews 7:12)

Here's how the law was changed:

> For the one concerning whom these things are spoken belongs to another tribe, from which no one has officiated at the altar. (Hebrews 7:13)

In His humanity, Jesus was not a descendant of the tribe of Levi; He was a descendant of Judah.

> For it is evident that our Lord was descended from Judah, a tribe with reference to which Moses spoke nothing concerning priests. And this is clearer still, if another priest arises according to the likeness of Melchizedek, (Hebrews 7:14–15)

The next verse explains this likeness:

> who has become such not on the basis of a law of physical requirement [that he had to be a Levite], but according to the power of an indestructible life. For it is attested of Him, "You are a priest forever according to the order of Melchizedek." (Hebrews 7:16–17)

Jesus became our high priest forever because of "the power of an indestructible life." The grave could not hold Him! Jesus died that we could be declared righteous even as we remain unrighteous and our imperfections (known as sins) could be forgiven. And it was His resurrection that propelled Him into His role as our high priest—He lives forever to be the only way that anyone can come to God the Father.

> For, on the one hand, there is a setting aside of a former commandment because of its weakness and uselessness (for the Law made nothing perfect), and on the other hand there is a bringing in of a better hope, through which we draw near to God. (Hebrews 7:18–19)

My wife read a book titled *The Seamstress*, by Sara Tuvel Bernstein. As she shared the story with me, I thought it illustrated how we work so hard to be right before God, or pave our own pathway to Him, and yet how misguided that mentality is.

The Seamstress is Ms. Bernstein's memoir as a Holocaust survivor. She told how her sister Esther and her friend Ellen were shipped via a train car straight into the heart of the war with all the bombings and machine guns firing. She feared for her life to the point of losing hope. Every night the door on the side of the car would be opened to take out the bodies of those who had died. In the four days they were on the train the numbers dwindled from about eighty women to twenty who were still alive.

When they stopped on the fourth day, Sara looked through a crack and saw a Red Cross truck and said, "Oh, girls! We're gonna get some food!" An SS Nazi soldier cracked open the door and immediately the air-raid siren went off. The soldier and the Red Cross officials ran for cover and the bombs began to fall. One of them hit the train car. Esther, Sara's sister, was hit in the back with some shrapnel—injured, but alive. The three of them got out of the train car and made their way into some nearby pine trees and hid out until night.

The rain began to fall and Ellen, Esther, and Sara walked across a field, to a farm and went to the barn. As they tried to open the door a man on the other side wouldn't let them in. But, when Sara pleaded with the man, stating that her sister was severely injured, he let them in. Through the darkness Sara could see, staring at her, all these white, bony faces of others who had escaped from the train also. The three women made their way through the crowded space and found a place to rest.

Six days later—after leaving the barn, rummaging for food, another explosion which killed many who were with them in the barn, and Esther who was getting worse and worse from her wounds—a white truck drove up to the barracks where they were; the men came up to them, speaking in a language they did not know, and tried to convince them to get into the white truck. "Absolutely not! We are not leaving with someone we don't know." Then a translator spoke for them— they were American soldiers who would take the women to a convent turned into a hospital. Sara was exhausted—the war was over? Sara, in her late twenties by this time weighed forty-four pounds. Once in the white truck, she closed her eyes. After about a fifty kilometer ride Sara felt herself being lifted up into two arms—one of the American soldiers was carrying her. As she lay there in his arms, eyes still closed, drops of water began to splash on her cheeks and ran down her neck. *It's raining again? No, we're inside—it can't be raining.* Then she realized the soldier who was carrying her was crying, his tears falling on her face.

Sara finally relaxed, rested, and released herself from the struggle; placed on a soft bed, in clean sheets, from the moment the soldier picked her up, she felt like she was in heaven.[49]

Here is how this story illustrates how we try to make our pathway to God and how that can be wrong: People have a deep drive to survive. We work so hard to rescue ourselves; we struggle through life and constantly work to make things right. For those who think about God, we have this urge to try to make ourselves right by our own

---

[49] Bernstein, *Seamstress*, 262–73.

efforts—we think we can save ourselves. What Sara and her sisters couldn't do for themselves those American soldiers did for them—they rescued them.

While we were yet sinners, God's compassion for us drove Him to send His Son to scoop us up, to rescue us, to carry us. The compassion of that American soldier for Sara reflects the heart of God for us. God desires to rescue us from our struggle: no more fighting for our own survival; just relax, rest, and release ourselves into His arms. He calls us into a relationship with Him: a relationship where we rely on Him to save us from the penalty of our sin (that's called justification), and a relationship where we rely on Him to rescue us from the power of sin in our lives (that's called sanctification).

When God saves us through His Son, He calls us to walk with Him, and He gives us the help we need to walk with Him. It is a pathway of companionship with Him, and at the same time, it is a path of reliance upon Him. This pathway is one where we can know God now.

Let's look again at Hebrews 7:19.

(for the Law made nothing perfect), and on the other hand there is a bringing in of a better hope, through which we draw near to God. (Hebrews 7:19)

We don't have to wait until we get to heaven to know God. We can draw near to Him now—through Jesus.

I was in a Bible study with some men, and one of the guys in the group said, "Bottom line: God loves you and He is for you, not against you." I'm not sure how many Christians really believe this, but it is true. God wants us to thrive, to have great marriages and great families, to know His joy right now, to experience His rest right now—to feel His arms carrying us even today. Christians will object by saying, "What about my struggles, pain, or hardship?" We all have them, yet those who cling to Jesus and seek Him to help them, and trust Him through the hardships, will know the abundant life. People I have known who have endured hardships and have clung to Jesus in the midst of them are some of the deepest Christians I've encountered. God seems to use those hard times to grow us deeper in our relationship with Him (just read James 1:2–4).

Not only is the pathway through Jesus about knowing God now, it is also about the hope we have for eternity.

> And inasmuch as it was not without an oath (for they indeed became priests without an oath, but He with an oath through the One who said to Him, "The Lord has sworn and will not change His mind, 'You are a priest forever'"); so much the more also Jesus has become the guarantee of a better covenant. (Hebrews 7:20–22)

The word "guarantee" is found only here in the Bible. It means "the collateral."[50] This better covenant will happen because Jesus is the collateral—He fulfilled the payment for this better covenant with His own life. This "better covenant" will be expanded upon in Hebrews 8. Yet, in short, it speaks of where the pathway is headed. This better covenant is headed to an eternity where we will all know the Lord as our God. Until then this pathway we are on is a journey where we know that the Lord Jesus is here to help us now.

> The former priests, on the one hand, existed in greater numbers because they were prevented by death from continuing, but Jesus, on the other hand, because He continues forever, holds His priesthood permanently. Therefore He is able also to save forever those who draw near to God through Him, since He always lives to make intercession for them. (Hebrews 7:23–25)

As our high priest right now, Jesus is able to "save forever those who draw near to God through Him." The word "forever" is another rarely used word in the Bible. The Greek word is *pantelles* and is found

---

[50] "In relationship to the covenant, Jesus is designated ἔγγυος, 'guarantor.' The choice of the term, which occurs only here in the NT, is purposeful. In the papyri it can denote a bond, a collateral, or some form of material guarantee that a debt will be paid or a promise fulfilled. But it may also refer to an individual who offers his own life as the guarantor of another person (see especially Sir 29:15–17). In this personal sense, the ἔγγυος assumes a weightier responsibility than the μεσίτης, 'mediator' (cf. 8:6; 9:15; 12:24). The 'mediator' steps into the gap between two parties, but the 'guarantor' stakes his person and his life on his word (cf. Michel, 275). Through his death, exaltation, and installation as heavenly priest, Jesus provides security that the new and better covenant will not be annulled." (Lane, *Hebrews 1–8*, 47A, S. 188).

only here and in Luke 13:11 where a woman could not straighten up *at all* ("at all" is the same Greek word). In extrabiblical works this word is found to mean "in all respects, finally, or completely." I think the NIV (New International Version) has the best translation of this verse: it translates *pantelles* as "completely."

To be saved by drawing near to God means God will remove whatever gets in our way of living the lives He desires for us. For example, things like our wrong attitudes, wrong actions, or our wrong thoughts and behaviors. Jesus saves us from the power of sin in all respects, finally, completely, so that we can draw near to God. Once again, the image of the soldier carrying Sara is good to recall. What we do is call on the Lord, come to His throne of grace (Hebrews 4:14–16), and let Him carry us. We must humble ourselves and seek His help, saying, "Lord, I need you! Lord, please help me."

What the author of Hebrews was getting at in this last half of Hebrews 7 was this: stop looking anywhere else; just look to Jesus!

When I was little (before first grade), I remember going with my family one winter to a park near our home called Whitnall Park. We got all bundled up, tied our toboggan on the luggage rack on top of the station wagon, and loaded everyone into the car. We were headed for a "toboggan chute." I didn't know what a toboggan chute was, but I knew what we did with our toboggan—we went sledding! So I was quite surprised when we got out of our car, walked over to the top of the toboggan chute, and stared at this trough with wooden sides and ice coating the bottom. The toboggan chute started at the top of the hill and shot down into the darkness. There was a man who was working as the "operator" at the top of the shoot. I remember he was working some kind of a lever that released each toboggan so that it could slide off into the abyss below. My dad threw the toboggan onto the ice in the trough. Everyone piled on and tried to urge me to do the same. I refused. They all smiled really big and tried to convince me it would be fun. There was no way I was getting on that toboggan, not when it was all set to go who-knows-where. I clung to the operator guy, screaming and crying, "Don't make me go." My parents and brothers and sisters all looked at the operator, a complete stranger, and asked if it would be okay if I stayed with him (that was back in the day when you wouldn't mind leaving your young child with a complete stranger—I guess). He agreed and then pulled the lever. My family quickly disappeared into the darkness. I could hear them screaming and then laughing in the darkness. It wasn't too long before they appeared back into the light as they made their way back up the hill. When they got back, they tried again to convince me to join them. "Come on, Jeremy, it's really fun!" I refused, and off they went for another ride. Finally, after their third or fourth time, they convinced me to try it out. I sat with my dad behind me and my mom in front of me. I looked up at the operator guy, who gave me a smile I wasn't sure how to interpret—was he happy for me, or did he know something I didn't? As he pulled the lever, the toboggan started out slow, but it wasn't long before we were flying down the chute. I gave my mom's coat the white-knuckle grip as I screamed. Then my fear turned into joy—this was a *blast*! We got to the bottom and shot across the field and then went zooming past others who had gone before us. I didn't want to stop! I wanted to go again, and maybe we could beat our record for how far we had gone. What I was afraid of at first ended up being a thrill.

I think the whole concept of looking to Jesus and not anywhere else is something that people are fearful of, because it means that we have to give up control and trust Him. It means that we may not know what exactly lies ahead, but we have to walk by faith. What if Jesus lets me down? What if He's not the answer; what if I go down the chute and end up in the abyss? Well, the author of Hebrews reminds us who Jesus is:

> For it was fitting for us to have such a high priest, holy, innocent, undefiled, separated from sinners and exalted above the heavens; who does not need daily, like those high priests, to offer up sacrifices, first for His own sins and then for the sins of the people, because this He did once for all when He offered up Himself. For the Law appoints men as high priests who are weak, but the word of the oath, which came after the Law, appoints a Son, made perfect forever. (Hebrews 7:26–28)

Jesus is the perfect pathway. All other pathways, no matter how devoted to them people are, are weak, useless (Hebrews 7:18), and wrong. To choose the pathway of Jesus is like choosing the ride of the toboggan chute: It may look scary, and our immediate reaction might be to cling to what we know. But if we place our lives in Jesus and trust Him even if we're not sure about it, if we surrender ourselves to Him, He will carry us, He will lead us, He will be our high priest who will make us complete before God. He will do for us what we cannot do for ourselves; He is the only way we can draw near to God. When we put all our trust in Jesus, we are embarking on a great and eternal journey.

CHAPTER TWELVE

WHAT'S UP IN HEAVEN?

Hebrews 8:1–6

The soldiers drove the nails through His hands and feet and let Him hang there to die. Jesus struggled for hours. Heavy clouds formed, darkening the sun. Finally, fighting for His life, He pushed out, "It is finished," bowed His head, exhaled, and breathed His last. All of heaven gasped…waited. Was that it? Would Jesus arise? Would He be returning to His eternal dwelling place? Was it over? Did God have a different plan for eternity? The beloved Son—was He gone forever?

On the third day as His body lay in the tomb, there was a blink, a twitch, a slight movement. Could it be? Yes, Jesus was alive! From one end of heaven to the other you could feel the excitement growing. All of eternity now would be changed. Jesus would physically return to heaven! Imagine the joy, the elation! It was absolutely immeasurable! Jesus would be coming back!

Forty days after the resurrection Jesus ascended into heaven. Have you ever wondered what Jesus has been doing up there? For about the last two thousand years has He been just waiting around for the rapture to occur? Has His role been limited to welcoming those who have passed from this life to that like a greeter at Wal-Mart or a hostess at a restaurant? Continuing through the book of Hebrews, we come to a passage that gives a glimpse into heaven. More specifically, it gives us a snapshot of what Jesus has been doing up there all these years.

The section of Hebrews we are in is all about Jesus as our high priest (Hebrews 7:1–10:25). It is good to note that Jesus is not just *a* high priest, but He is *our* high priest. Notice, specifically, that Hebrews 8:1 says, "We have…"

> Now the main point in what has been said is this: *we have* such a high priest, who has taken His seat at the right hand of the throne of the Majesty in the heavens… (Hebrews 8:1)

Jesus is a high priest who is available to us now. He has become a high priest *for us*! Even though He is in heaven, we are on His mind and in His heart.

We can also note from Hebrews 8:1 that Jesus is in the place of highest honor in heaven.

> Now the main point in what has been said is this: we have such a high priest, *who has taken His seat at the right hand of the throne* of the Majesty in the heavens… (Hebrews 8:1)

When you and I sit down, it can mean a lot of things: sometimes we are exhausted, so we sit down to take a break. Other times we sit down to be stubborn and say either outwardly or in our minds, "I'm not moving." Sometimes we sit down to protest in a peaceful way, like planting ourselves in front of a public building to make a statement. We sit down to have fellowship with others around the dinner table. Where we sit can be an indication of prestige or authority. Some families always have dad at the head of the table. A leader or a dignitary will often sit at the head of the table. Sitting communicates a lot of things. When someone sits down at the right hand of the king, it communicates there is no one in the entire kingdom who has a higher status. God the Father sits on the throne, with Jesus, His Son, at His right hand (Ephesians 1:17–20). And did you notice that Jesus took "*His* seat" (Hebrews 8:1)? No one else can occupy that position.

Not only is Jesus in the place of highest honor, He is also at the center of supreme authority.

> Now the main point in what has been said is this: we have such a high priest, who has taken His seat at the right hand of the throne *of the Majesty* in the heavens… (Hebrews 8:1)

The title "Majesty" indicates that God has sovereign power and therefore is completely in charge. It also means that Jesus rules over everyone from the realm of ultimate glory.

> Now the main point in what has been said is this: we have such a high priest, who has taken His seat at the right hand of the throne of the Majesty *in the heavens,* (Hebrews 8:1)

Notice that "heavens" is plural. Sometimes in the English translations, the plural is translated in the singular, while other times it is translated in the plural.[51] Here in Hebrews 8:1 it does not mean more than one heaven; it is an expression of the magnitude, glory, and splendor of heaven. It speaks of the vastness of heaven and the spectacular nature of heaven. It is the place where Jesus is in His physical form right now.

Jesus is there on the throne as the leader in the purest and most refined place of worship.

> a minister in the sanctuary and in the true tabernacle, which the Lord pitched, not man. (Hebrews 8:2)

Have you ever considered that Jesus is a minister? There are three different Greek words for "minister."[52] The Greek word used here is *leitourgos.* In the Septuagint (the ancient Greek translation of the Old Testament) this same Greek word almost always refers to the priests working in the tabernacle or temple. We get our English word "liturgy" from *leitourgos.* The liturgy is that which governs worship (typically in traditional or liturgical churches). Jesus governs, or presides over, worship in heaven. I find it somewhat mind-boggling that the One who we will bow our knees to in worship will actually lead us in worship as well.

Another interesting observation is the "true tabernacle" had a starting point:

---

[51] All of these are the plural form of "heavens" in Greek, but most are translated in the singular; for example, Matthew 5:12, 16; 6:1, 9; 16:19 (both plural); Luke 10:20; Ephesians 3:15; Philippians 3:20; Colossians 1:20 (in Colossians 1:16 the same word is translated in the plural). In Hebrews it is translated both as plural and singular (9:23; 12:23).

[52] *Leitourgos, hupeeretes,* and the most common, *diakonos.*

a minister in the sanctuary and in the true tabernacle, *which the Lord pitched*, not man. (Hebrews 8:2)

God made it—He *pitched* it, or set it up—so that His created beings would have a place to gather to worship Him while they are in heaven. Today, we go to places in order to worship the Lord together. These places of worship serve as copies of the true tabernacle. Churches throughout history have spent a lot of money to make their places of worship beautiful. By the architecture and decor, they give hints or paint a picture of the true sanctuary and true tabernacle in heaven. God has created a physical place in heaven so that physical beings (you and I) could worship Him there.

You may be thinking that this is all so lofty and it may sound really good, but do you believe it is true? The recipients of this letter never saw Jesus glorified in heaven. These two verses paint the scene in heaven and no one on earth can see it right now. So how can we believe it?

There are many things that we have not seen firsthand that we believe exist. For instance, I asked for a show of hands in our church for those who had actually seen the queen of England, Queen Elizabeth, and no one raised their hand. So I showed them a picture of her and mentioned that there was video evidence that she existed and we had heard of eyewitness accounts, which established the facts. Based on what we had seen and heard, everyone in the congregation believed that Queen Elizabeth does exist.

Here are the facts that have been gathered about Jesus: He appeared to over five hundred people after His resurrection and before His ascension. He told them that He was going to heaven and that one day He would be returning. He often talked about His going to the right hand of God the Father in heaven. Some saw Him ascend into heaven. The authors of the New Testament were all convinced He was there. The apostle Paul and the apostle John even saw Him in His glorified state. All but one of the apostles were martyred for their commitment to this truth. The facts are clear and the witnesses have shared what they have seen; now we have the freedom to either trust the facts or dismiss them.

I am convinced and have chosen to believe that Jesus is in heaven as our high priest. The reason He is our high priest is because He offered the holiest sacrifice to God on our behalf: Himself.

> For every high priest is appointed to offer both gifts and sacrifices; so it is necessary that this high priest also have something to offer. Now if He were on earth, He would not be a priest at all, since there are those who offer the gifts according to the Law... (Hebrews 8:3–4)

In the Old Testament the law went into great detail about what gift or sacrifice was to be offered for different sins or offenses. But Jesus offered Himself, and there is nothing in the law that says anything about Jesus offering Himself as the perfect sacrifice. Yet Jesus is the perfect gift and sacrifice to God for our sins because every person falls short of God's glory and holy perfection. What the priests of the Old Testament did was just a copy of the real and only sacrifice that could pay the full price and penalty for our sin.

> Now if He were on earth, He would not be a priest at all, since there are those who offer the gifts according to the Law; *who serve a copy and shadow* of the heavenly things, just as Moses was warned by God when he was about to erect the tabernacle; for, "See," He says, "that you make all things according to the pattern which was shown you on the mountain." (Hebrews 8:4–5)

I think it is somewhat fascinating and very important to take us back to that time when Moses went up on the mountain and saw the pattern of the true tabernacle.

- Look at what was happening as Moses went up on the mountain with Aaron, Joshua, and seventy elders: "Then Moses went up with Aaron, Nadab and Abihu, and seventy of the elders of Israel, and they saw the God of Israel; and under His feet there appeared to be a pavement of sapphire, as clear as the sky itself. Yet He did not stretch out His hand against the nobles of the sons of Israel; and they saw God, and they ate and drank" (Exodus 24:9–11).

- Then, when Moses went up on the mountain, he got an extra measure of seeing the glory of God: "Then Moses went up to the mountain, and the cloud covered the mountain. The glory of the LORD rested on Mount Sinai, and the cloud covered it for six days; and on the seventh day He called to Moses from the midst of the cloud. And to the eyes of the sons of Israel the appearance of the glory of the LORD was like a consuming fire on the mountain top. Moses entered the midst of the cloud as he went up to the mountain; and Moses was on the mountain forty days and forty nights" (Exodus 24:15–18).

- And it was from that glory that he was given, by God, the pattern to make the tabernacle: "According to all that I am going to show you, as the pattern of the tabernacle and the pattern of all its furniture, just so you shall construct it" (Exodus 25:9). "See that you make them after the pattern for them, which was shown to you on the mountain" (Exodus 25:40).

The reason for all the detail (as seen in Leviticus) in connection to the tabernacle and its service was because it had to reflect Christ, "picturing His glorious person and His wondrous work. This was why God was so particular in regard to all its details."[53] Moses was not given any creative license; he had to put the tabernacle together in all its detail right down to the bowls that would be used, all according to God's design. I'm convinced that Moses, on Mount Sinai, saw the true tabernacle and made the earthly one in its likeness.

I live a little over an hour north of Milwaukee, Wisconsin. So when the Milwaukee Public Museum had the Dead Sea Scrolls on exhibit, a group of us from our church went to see them. As we walked through the exhibit, we saw amazing ancient artifacts from biblical times. Things like pottery, inkwells, even ossuaries (containers where human bones were stored). This was all to whet our appetite for the main course—some of the Dead Sea Scrolls themselves! As the people funneled into the room where the scrolls were on display, they came to the first exhibit, which held the longest intact scroll in existence (I believe it was the entire book of Isaiah).

As I waited in line for about an hour, I looked at the photographs and read the descriptions on the walls that talked about the Dead Sea Scrolls in general and about this very long scroll specifically. I read that it measured about eight meters in length, where it was found, along with other fascinating facts. But finally, I got up to the glass case

---

[53] Ironside, *Hebrews*, 74.

where the scroll was rolled out. Oh, I had to get a good look. I had to see if I could decipher any of the words. I had to see what the notes said about it as I slowly made my way down that eight-meter case. As I read the notes, I kept noticing a common word that described this long scroll. They kept saying things like "This facsimile..." and "the facsimile..." and "a rare facsimile." So I finally inquired to one of the workers, "What does it mean, 'facsimile'?" And the man said, "Oh, this is a copy of the actual scroll, like getting a facsimile in your office." It felt like someone had just popped my balloon. Here I had waited in this long line with such great anticipation, and all I got to see was a copy? Well, at least the rest of the exhibit had actual, *real*, fragments of the Dead Sea Scrolls, and I was very impressed with them.

The tabernacle that Moses had made was, no doubt, an amazing place of worship. Some church buildings in our world today are amazing places of worship as well. But they are attempts at "facsimiles" of the real thing. I have a feeling, when we see the original, it will take our breath away! And the One who is and will be leading worship there...I can't even imagine what it will be like being under His leadership!

Jesus reigns supreme in His ministry from heaven because He, and He alone, is the mediator between God and us.

> But now He has *obtained* a more excellent ministry, by as much as He is also the mediator of a *better covenant*... (Hebrews 8:6a)

When the Bible says that Jesus is the mediator, I think He does this on two levels. Notice first of all that Jesus "obtained" this ministry. He fulfilled every requirement of the law. He lived up to all the conditions of the old covenant of the law. Then, to install "a better covenant," Jesus died on the cross to pay the penalty for our sins, sealing a covenant of forgiveness where our sins are not held against us. The second way in which Jesus mediates for us is by interceding for us over and over again when He talks with God the Father on our behalf. We see a picture of this in John 17 when Jesus prayed for His disciples and for us. He prayed that His joy would be made full in us and that we would be kept from evil and grow in holiness and in the truth. What He did then, I'm confident He does now: He sees our lives and hears our prayers and He mediates—He converses with the Father on our behalf.

The ministry of Jesus (which He conducts from heaven) for us is a ministry based on His promises, not our performance.

> But now He has obtained a more excellent ministry, by as much as He is also the mediator of a better covenant, *which has been enacted on better promises.* (Hebrews 8:6)

The old promises were out of the law. For example, Exodus 19:5 states, "Now then, if you will indeed obey My voice and keep My covenant, then you shall be My own possession among all the peoples, for all the earth is Mine." Another way to say this is "If you perform, you will experience God's blessings." That was then. Now God works in us by sending His Holy Spirit to indwell us. It is the Holy Spirit who is our seal and the promise that God is near. Today, God is within us. God has promised to give us eternal life, a relationship with Him as our Father that starts today and lasts forever.

Years ago I was awakened at around 3:00 a.m. to the phone ringing. I mumbled a hello only to hear a very awake and straightforward voice on the other end say, "Mark and Charlotte's house is on fire!" Mark is one of my best friends. He and his wife, Charlotte, and their two girls lived on the street behind our house about three doors down. I ran to the back of our house, looked out the window, and saw the night sky glowing orange from the flames. I threw on some clothes and ran out of the house, telling my wife, Jill, that I would call her when I knew what was up. I hurried through the backyards and over to where the fire trucks were dowsing the engulfed house. I found Mark, Charlotte, their two girls, and even their dog, Molly. They had all made it out safely. Sadly, however, all of us, including Mark's mom, his siblings, and the neighbors, could only watch as almost all of their earthly possessions literally went up in smoke. We were helpless to do anything.

By the crack of dawn we were able to begin to go into the blackened house to see what could be salvaged. The role that I found myself playing was the counselor, making sure people were all right. I cried with some, prayed with others, all the while talking with those there who needed someone to process this tragedy. I kept my composure, holding it together...that is until I went back home at about 9:00 a.m. As soon as I walked in the door, Jill met me, and I lost it. I just started crying; I couldn't handle the load. It was just such a heavy night, and I felt so bad. I knew that the well-being of Mark and his family was not ultimately on my shoulders, but feeling like I was carrying it, even for that little while, was too much for me to bear.

As a pastor, sometimes I feel like the well-being of the believers in our church is on my shoulders. As Christians, we may feel that our well-being as followers of Christ is on our own shoulders. However, ultimately, our well-being as Christians falls on the shoulders of Jesus. Right now, Jesus is in charge of our experience with Him and growth in Him. Every Christian can know God as their Father because of what Jesus did for them, and what He does for them even now as their mediator. The way we tap into what Jesus has for us is through faith— in which we trust in Him, rely on Him, and place our confidence in Him as we seek to follow Him.

Our eternal destiny is secured by Jesus. When we get to heaven, as He sits on the throne ruling in perfect righteousness and leading us in worship, we will know that Jesus is in charge.

I don't know about you, but I am glad He's the One who carries that burden (so we don't have to). How does that hit you? If you're like me, it makes you want to know Him more, serve Him better, and bring Him the honor and the glory that only He—*who has taken His seat at the right hand of the throne of the Majesty in the heavens*—deserves.

CHAPTER THIRTEEN

WE CAN'T—WE WILL—BUT UNTIL

Hebrews 8:6–13

I don't know how much you know about music, but a simple C scale consists of the notes C, D, E, F, G, A, B, C. If I played a C scale and left out the last note (the final C) it would sound almost the way it should; we would know that it sounded right...except for the missing final note. The scale would feel incomplete or unresolved. If you heard it played, it would probably make you want to hit that unstruck note yourself.

Are you like me? We know Jesus said that if we are to pursue Him, know Him, live for Him, we must deny ourselves, take up our cross *daily*, and follow Him (Luke 9:23). But I get distracted, I get tired, and I don't always know exactly what it means to follow Him in certain circumstances. It's like I want to follow Him fully, but I often have a hard time hitting that final note.

As we highlighted earlier the whole book of Hebrews is about how to be companions with our Lord Jesus Christ. The Greek word that is threaded throughout the book is *metochoi* (Hebrews 1:9; 3:1 14, 6:4), which means being "partners," "companions," or "partakers." If you have been following this book so far, you might be saying, "Yes, I want to be a companion with Jesus. I want to be His partner in what He's doing in this world. I'm looking forward to partaking in His will forever." I would also guess that 100 percent of those who said, "Yes," have struggles similar to mine. We are not alone. Even the recipients of the letter of Hebrews struggled with how to live this way with Christ in a consistent way. So, with a pastor's heart, the author of Hebrews helped those first-century Jewish Christians (who were somewhat young in their faith) to understand how this companionship with Jesus works.

The author started by telling them we can't live for the Lord doing things the old way. He understood that these Christians had come out of Judaism. They had lived their whole lives believing in the law, which God gave to Israel through Moses. They had believed in the Old Testament priesthood, so the author strove to realign their thinking with the role Jesus plays as their high priest. The Jewish Christians knew what the Pentateuch (the first five books of the Old Testament) said about how people would align themselves to become companions with God. So the author of Hebrews stepped in, trying to help them see that the old way never worked. In this next section he explained there would be a new way to be companions with God the Father and the Lord Jesus Christ.

> But now He has obtained a more excellent ministry, by as much as He is also the mediator of a better covenant, which has been enacted on better promises. For if that first covenant had been faultless, there would have been no occasion sought for a second. (Hebrews 8:6–7)

That "first covenant" was the covenant God made with Israel through Moses. It was the contract the Israelites had agreed to. They would obey the law and therefore be the people of God. But that old way had some flaws. To produce people who would consistently draw near to God, who would know Him and serve Him, the first covenant was not going to work.

> For if that first covenant had been faultless, there would have been no occasion sought for a second. (Hebrews 8:7)

Back when I was in college, I worked for the Orange City, Iowa, Park and Recreation Department. I taught golf to children who were between the ages of eight and twelve years old. The hardest kids to teach were those who had been playing golf for a while, because they had picked up some bad habits. So when I would tell them to grip the club a certain way, or stand a certain way, or place the ball at a certain place between their feet, they would say things like, "That doesn't feel right," or, "I don't like that." And they would go back to their old ways.

We can pick up some bad habits in our Christian traditions, and trying to change them *just doesn't feel right*. A popular bad habit in golf is picking up your head when you swing at the ball. A popular bad habit in Christianity is thinking we just have to work harder or put more restrictions in place. Another way to say it is, we just have to draw the line darker and clarify the law better and work more diligently at keeping it. Then, we feel, we will be the Lord's companions. But here's a secret—it will never work. In golf, when you pick up your head before hitting the ball, you will always top the ball or fail to hit the ball where you want it to go. In Christianity, focusing on our actions in the course of wanting to partner with Christ will result in not becoming the companions we desire to be. The result will be that we will feel either like failures or like Pharisees (thinking that we're pretty great, even acting pompous). Neither way is good.

To get to the point of this new way of being Christ's companions today, the author of Hebrews looked ahead to the future and pointed out that there is coming a day when the Jewish people, the Israelites, will be the Lord's companions because they will be living in a new way.

> For finding fault with them, He says, "Behold, days are coming, says the Lord, when I will effect a new covenant with the house of Israel and with the house of Judah; (Hebrews 8:8)[54]

This quote is the beginning of the longest Old Testament quote in the New Testament. It is a prophecy that lays out the new way, which is called the "new covenant" and is quoted from Jeremiah 31:31–34. It is one of the many prophecies that indicate that God's plan for Israel is not over. Yet, according to Romans 11:17–22, like wild olive branches being grafted into an olive tree, Christians who are not Jewish have

---

[54] In Israelite history there was a time when the kingdom was divided. Israel was to the north, and Judah was to the south. But they were all one people—the Israelites.

been grafted into the rich roots of God's eternal plans that He has for Israel.

> not like the covenant which I made with their fathers on the day when I took them by the hand to lead them out of the land of Egypt; for they did not continue in My covenant, and I did not care for them, says the Lord. (Hebrews 8:9)

It may strike us the wrong way thinking that God "did not care for them." This can also be translated, "I disregarded them." God let them have their way: They did not continue in the covenant, in the agreement; they did not want God's care for them, so God let them go to their desired end—far away from Him. But God would make a new covenant through the prophet Jeremiah. It would be a new agreement that was not reliant upon the ability of the people, but solely reliant upon the work of the Lord.

Along with Israel, God will make Christians of one mind, set on Him.

> For this is the covenant that I will make with the house of Israel after those days, says the Lord: I will put My laws into their minds, and I will write them on their hearts. And I will be their God, and they shall be My people. (Hebrews 8:10)

The New American Standard Bible reads, "I will put My laws into their minds." Actually the word "minds" is singular—"mind." The King James Version and the New King James Version translate it correctly, keeping it in the singular. This quote from Jeremiah says that God will put His laws into *their* (plural) *mind* (singular). I believe this is saying there is coming a day when each person will be a part of the collective mind-set, being united in knowing the Lord and living for Him. At the same time, God will make each and every one of us who are His children have a heart for Him. The word "hearts" in Hebrews 8:10 is in the plural. This shows our individuality. While we will have perfect unity, we will keep our individuality and our uniqueness. The Lord created you to be you and me to be me. There will never be another one like you, and within that uniqueness one day, without hindrance or barriers, you and I will love the Lord with all our hearts.

> And they shall not teach everyone his fellow citizen, and everyone his brother, saying, 'Know the Lord,' for all will know Me, from the least to the greatest of them. (Hebrews 8:11)

Did you happen to watch the royal wedding of William and Kate, who are now the Duke and Duchess of Cambridge? It was estimated that two billion people watched. I have three daughters and a wife who watched it; therefore, I found myself sitting through it as well. As I watched the ceremony, honestly, I was feeling a little cynical. I remember watching Charles and Diana back in 1981 when they said similar vows. If you know their history, you know how tragically that turned out. I was asking myself how much William and Kate will actually commit their lives to God the Father, God the Son, and God the Holy Ghost as the archbishop of Canterbury told them to do while he led the ceremony. I was wondering how much their marriage will be committed to Christ in order to be a reflection of Christ and the church as the archbishop pronounced they ought. I realize I don't know the couple and may never know how much they will honor those admonitions. I also realize, especially for my daughters, that this was a fairy-tale wedding and therefore coming into our living room for its entertainment value, not for spiritual nurturing.

Yet we know, by the authority of the Bible, and the verse mentioned above, there is coming a day when all—from the least to the greatest, from commoners to kings—will know the Lord and will truly be committed to loving and honoring Him. In that day, God will make our existence sinless. No longer will there be all the junk in our world that sin has produced.

> For I will be merciful to their iniquities, and I will remember their sins no more." (Hebrews 8:12)

You and I sin, and we know that through Christ we are forgiven. However, we are not out of the woods yet. We live in a sin-soaked world. We have hearts that are easily lured away from the Lord. We have a tendency to drift away from the One who saved us (hence the warning in Hebrews 2:1). Let's face it; a war is being waged, and like it or not, we are in it. But there is coming a day when the existence of sin will be no more.

And I heard a loud voice from the throne, saying, "Behold, the tabernacle of God is among men, and He will dwell among them, and they shall be His people, and God Himself will be among them, and He will wipe away every tear from their eyes; and there will no longer be any death; there will no longer be any mourning, or crying, or pain; the first things have passed away." And He who sits on the throne said, "Behold, I am making all things new." And He said, "Write, for these words are faithful and true." (Revelation 21:3–5)

This will happen—a new day and a new way!

But what about now? Up to this point we have talked about how *we can't* (not the old way), but *we will* (some day) be unhindered in our partnership with Jesus. What about now *until* that future glory? Can we be the Lord's companions today? We can because of His grace. The eighth chapter of Hebrews ends with these words:

When He said, "A new covenant," He has made the first obsolete. But whatever is becoming obsolete and growing old is ready to disappear. (Hebrews 8:13)

What this verse mentions about the old covenant is one of my fears for my own life: that I am going to grow old and become obsolete or irrelevant. Some people grow old and become crotchety or grumpy. Others are nice, but they are graciously put out to pasture. I don't like either of those options.

I was at a pastor's conference a number of years ago, and a part of the program was a group of leaders within our denomination were to stand up and each one was given time to speak. There was a man on the panel who was clearly the oldest one on the platform. He wore a cardigan sweater and baggy grayish brown pants, and he sat there with rounded shoulders. I wondered what he could have to contribute to the program. Honestly, I thought, *Well, he must have some history with our denomination and they are just being nice to him by allowing him to be up there.* I thought I would just have to be gracious to him and let him share what was on his mind. He was introduced as Dr. Thomas McDill, the president of our denomination from 1976–1990. He sauntered up to the lectern and began to speak. When he opened his mouth, I was captivated! He was sharp, witty, articulate, intelligent, and so gracious. As I listened to him, I couldn't help feeling like I wanted to be like him *when I grow up*. Unlike Dr. McDill, the old covenant is becoming obsolete. Yet notice that it is only "ready to disappear." The implication is that it isn't gone yet.

When I was a senior in college, I went on a four-day hiking trip with my friend Brent through the Rocky Mountains. It was quite the trip. As we walked along the path, we noticed a summit that would bring us above the tree line. Enticed, we decided to veer off the path and climb the summit. As we got a closer look at it, we realized there were two tiers to it. We thought we could climb up to the first tier, see how much daylight we had, and then make our way up the second tier to the snowcapped summit (even though it was July). When we made it to the top of the first tier, we saw something we hadn't noticed: a large valley separated the two tiers, making the mountain appear to have two summits and that the one we had climbed was just shorter. To the saints of the Old Testament, the two summits of the old covenant and the new covenant were seen as two tiers (one right after the other). But the reality is a valley has existed between the two ever since the time Jesus walked this earth. We are living in this valley right now; we can call it the valley of grace, or the age of grace, or the church age.

This is a time when we can draw near to the Lord because of His grace to us. All throughout the book of Hebrews the author has been telling his readers to draw near to the Lord, that we have a high priest who is gentle and who sympathizes with our weaknesses. He is near and is ready to minister to us. But in this life, it doesn't come naturally—like it will when we experience the new covenant with the Lord in the future kingdom.

We are living in this middle valley. On the one hand, the effects of the law have not disappeared yet, because, much as the law was to be obeyed by an act of the will, drawing near to our Lord is an act of our will. In the future kingdom, it won't even be a choice. As angels naturally obey the Lord and are in His service, we will do likewise. But we live in a world that constantly battles against that. Therefore, we have to choose to follow the Lord (Luke 9:23). On the other hand, like the new covenant is an act of God transforming us, God has sent His Holy Spirit to be in us—to lead us and mold us. So today it is both an act of our will and a work of God.

I really believe that Jesus wants us to live lives that are not full of frustration and disappointment. I think He wants us to live lives that allow us to see Him actively working in them so we know that our lives count for Him and our lives, even today, are clearly unexplainable apart from Him because we live by faith. Jesus wants us to live our lives knowing that one day our lives will be complete, living out the new covenant without any hindrance of a fallen world, or a fallen nature. It will be a time when our collective mind and each of our hearts will be at ease with our Lord. When that day comes, our lives will feel like a complete C scale: C, D, E, F, G, A, B, C.

CHAPTER FOURTEEN

THE HEIGHT OF HOLINESS

Hebrews 9:1–14

O ver the years, I have watched people show their connection to the Lord. Often I will see them expressing the importance of their relationship with the Lord through the T-shirts they wear. Back in the '70s and '80s some wore T-shirts that had the phrase "Jesus Freak" pasted across the front. In the '80s and '90s it was common to see "WWJD" ("What Would Jesus Do") not only on T-shirts, but also on rubber bracelets and jewelry. Later, a popular TV commercial asked the question, "Got milk?" which led to T-shirts that said, "Got Jesus?" Shortly after the year 2000, particularly among teenagers, the T-shirts associating them with the Lord read, "Jesus is my homeboy."

I realize these Christians were trying to communicate a personal connection to Jesus. But I wonder if something might have gotten lost in those expressions over the decades. A sense of the holiness, sacredness, purity, separateness, and utter rightness of God lost its luster. God is so good, loving, gracious, and forgiving, yet are we awestruck enough by His holy perfection?

In the time of the Old Testament, when the Israelites had the tabernacle (and then the temple), they knew more than anything else how holy God was. When the Israelite priests entered the tabernacle and approached the bronze altar to make sacrifices, they felt intimidated and nervous. They wanted to be near God, yet they knew they could never approach Him. God was too otherworldly, too high up, and too pure for them. The Old Testament is clear: God was there in the tabernacle dwelling in the middle of His people and He was perfectly holy.

As we continue through the book of Hebrews, we need to remember that the author was writing to the first generation of Jewish Christians with the intention to move their hearts and minds from Judaism into Christianity, their connection from Jewish traditions into a companionship with Christ. He wanted to break them away from the old covenant (the law) and unite them with the new covenant (grace). A similar challenge we face today is to persuade people away from a religion into a relationship with Christ.

Hebrews 9 begins by describing the tabernacle.

> Now even the first covenant had regulations of divine worship and the earthly sanctuary. For there was a tabernacle prepared, the outer one, in which were the lampstand and the table and the sacred bread; this is called the holy place. Behind the second veil there was a tabernacle which is called the Holy of Holies, having a golden altar of incense and the ark of the covenant covered on all sides with gold, in which was a golden jar holding the manna, and Aaron's rod which budded, and the tables of the covenant; (Hebrews 9:1–4)

The most important piece of furniture in the tabernacle was the ark of the covenant. The most important items inside the ark were the tablets of the covenant. Those were the two pieces of stone where the Ten Commandments were written. The Ten Commandments defined, in a very succinct way, what holiness looked like. As you see from these verses, the ark of the covenant was found in the holy of holies. This was the place tucked in the very depths of the tabernacle like a hidden place of holiness: it was the place where God dwelled with His people. There is no other place that can be called holy apart from God. God defines holiness; God is holiness. Therefore, wherever God dwells is the place that can properly be called the place of holiness.

> and above it were the cherubim of glory overshadowing the mercy seat; but of these things we cannot now speak in detail. (Hebrews 9:5)

Did you notice how the description came to an abrupt end? It may sound odd; however, the author described all the details of the tabernacle in order to bring us to this very place—the mercy seat, the place where God resided. The holiness of God was too powerful, too intense for anyone to even live if they were in God's presence there. Therefore, where God resided was always hidden, tucked away behind the veil. A human being could not see the holiness of God and survive. The place where God was—the holy place—was hidden to protect the unholy person from being destroyed by it. I wonder, in this day and age, if we have we lost some of the reverence for God's holiness.

Someone might ask, "Why was it off-limits? Why couldn't people approach God in that holy of holies?" What was the hurdle that people could not get over in order to get to the place of holiness? In reality, it wasn't *totally* off-limits. It was true that no one was allowed into the holy of holies…except one person.

> Now when these things have been so prepared, the priests are continually entering the outer tabernacle performing the divine worship, but into the second, only the high priest enters once a year, not without taking blood, which he offers for himself and for the sins of the people committed in ignorance. (Hebrews 9:6–7)

Once a year, on a day called "the Day of Atonement," one man entered the holy of holies, and only for a brief time. He would go in and sprinkle the blood of a bull or goat on the mercy seat to bring harmony between God and His people again, to reconcile and restore peace. If he did anything wrong (from the way he dressed, to the type of incense he would burn, to the way in which he sacrificed the goat or bull for the blood to sprinkle on the seat (Leviticus 16:3–17), his very life was in jeopardy. These rituals and the regulations were passed down from one generation to the next to be performed annually as a function of the high priest. It revealed that the way to the most holy place—the way to God—was blocked.

The average person could not draw near to the Lord because the real hurdle was (and is) in the heart. We don't have pure hearts. We may think, *I am not a bad person*; however, in our hearts we will choose to not do the right things when we think the wrong we do is not that bad. It's like our hearts are broken, and try as we might, we can't seem to fix them.

> The Holy Spirit is signifying this, that the way into the holy place has not yet been disclosed while the outer tabernacle is still standing, which is a symbol for the present time. Accordingly both gifts and sacrifices are offered which cannot make the worshiper perfect in conscience... (Hebrews 9:8–9)

The only way we can enter into the place where God dwells is by having our consciences made perfect. You and I could do all the right stuff, but it wouldn't get at the heart of the issue. We could bring our sacrifices and gifts and do everything required in the Law, and we would still end up in the same place. Deep down you and I would know, "I'm not right with God; I'm not connected with Him." That is why the author of Hebrews wrote:

> which is a symbol for the present time. *Accordingly both gifts and sacrifices are offered which cannot make the worshiper perfect in conscience...* (Hebrews 9:9)

As I was growing up, my family had a wood-burning furnace. It sat next to our conventional forced-air furnace. We would burn wood all winter to keep the fuel cost down and our house warm. The wood we burned came from pallets we received from some of my parents' friends. With plenty of pallets regularly leftover from the company these friends owned, they told us we could take as many as we wanted. So we would load up our trailer with pallets and haul them to our house. While we piled up stacks of pallets at our house, I had a brilliant idea: I wanted to make a fort in our back woods behind the pasture and thought those pallets would be great wood to use. The only problem was I didn't think my dad would let me. So I decided to take some pallets without asking. I got our wheelbarrow and loaded up as many as I could and tried to quickly get back behind the barn and head to the woods without being seen. But the heavy wheelbarrow slipped out of my hands, and the pallets slid off and slammed down on my foot. Oh, that hurt. I couldn't help but limp. I tried avoiding my parents, but when my dad came home, one of the first things he said was, "Why are you limping? What's wrong with your foot?"

I tried to avoid answering the question, saying, "Oh, nothing."

I tried to be nice and relate to my dad, acting like nothing was wrong between us. But it was too much; I knew deep down I was not right with my dad. I knew he would figure it out. I finally told him that I took the pallets without asking. We talked it through, and he accepted my apology. Looking back, in confessing that I had stolen those pallets and talking to my dad about it, I did all the right stuff. But deep down inside I still felt guilty.

My action of taking those pallets without asking brought about my guilt, yet my action of confession did not alleviate my guilt. If the old way God operated was still in effect (the old covenant which was the way of the law), I know there would not be a week that went by (or even a day) that I would not continue to feel guilty, even if I had done all the right stuff according to the law. This is true because my heart (and your heart) cannot connect with God through the rites, rituals, and liturgy laid out in the law, or in our day it would be the equivalent of going through the motions of religion. Practicing religion will never get us over the hurdle of our hearts. There was and is a need for a new way.

> Accordingly both gifts and sacrifices are offered which cannot make the worshiper perfect in conscience, since they relate only to food and drink and various washings, regulations for the body imposed until a time of reformation. (Hebrews 9:9b–10)

The old ways were there "until a time of reformation." The time of reformation was an age for improvement, a new order, a new time, a new way in which God would work. The new way would remove the hidden place of holiness and create a highway to the place of holiness—an expressway, the only way! And the name of that highway is "Jesus"! Jesus breaks the barriers.

> But when Christ appeared as a high priest of the good things to come, He entered through the greater and more perfect tabernacle, not made with hands, that is to say, not of this creation; and not through the blood of goats and calves, but through His own blood, He entered the holy place once for all, having obtained eternal redemption. (Hebrews 9:11–12)

Jesus did not enter the holy place year after year like the high priests, and not with the blood of imperfect animals, but with His own perfect blood. When Jesus died, the veil leading into the holy of holies was torn from top to bottom (Matthew 27:51; Mark 15:38; Luke 23:45). You may remember that the veil was six inches thick. It's as though Jesus tore through all the heavy weight of the rules, regulations, and rites. He is the only perfect sacrifice to enter into the perfect tabernacle in heaven before God the Father. He is the only and perfect way, the highway to God. It is Jesus and Jesus alone who liberates. The chains are torn off, the weight of performance for acceptance is gone! The bondage of sin, the darkness, and the inability, no matter how hard we try, to measure up to all the regulations is destroyed.

> and not through the blood of goats and calves, but through His own blood, He entered the holy place once for all, *having obtained eternal redemption.* (Hebrews 9:12)

The word "redemption" means "paying to free the prisoner or captive."

In October 2010, thirty-three miners were trapped 2,040 feet (approximately a half mile) below the surface of the earth in Chile, South America. Seven hundred thousand tons of rock had collapsed and entombed them. For seventeen days those workers who were trapped didn't know if anyone knew they were alive. Then they heard the vibration of a drill bit coming into their small, dark, wet prison. As soon as the drill pierced the rock, they began to tap on it. When the drill stopped, they attached a note that said all thirty-three were alive. It would take an additional fifty-two days before the miners would be rescued. The escape capsule that was designed for such a time as this was thirteen feet tall and twenty-eight inches wide. One by one each of the miners were lifted out of the darkness, out of certain death and into the light. The president of Chile, Sebastián Piñera, told Victor Segovia, the fifteenth miner to emerge, "Welcome to life." Priscilla Avalos said when her brother came up, "It's as if [he] had been born again." The estimated cost for the rescue was about $22 million.[55]

For all the people who ever walked this planet, or ever will, Jesus made it possible for us to be saved out of our entombment of sin,

---

[55] Associated Press, "All 33 Chilean Miners."

darkness, and death. He rescues us one by one into His light. The cost for such a rescue: His own death. Jesus shed His own blood. The payment was eternal. Its value and our redemption are eternal. When we place our faith in Jesus as our one and only Savior, He lifts us out of our darkness, and God the Father says, in a sense, "Welcome to life." We are born again and forever saved!

> So if the Son makes you free, you will be free indeed. (John 8:36)

Here is how He does it: Jesus, through the Spirit, cleanses our hearts.

> For if the blood of goats and bulls and the ashes of a heifer sprinkling those who have been defiled sanctify for the cleansing of the flesh, how much more will the blood of Christ, who through the eternal Spirit offered Himself without blemish to God, cleanse your conscience from dead works to serve the living God? (Hebrews 9:13–14)

I love the contrast: outward actions versus inward passions; outward behaviors versus inward motivators; outward duties versus inward desires. The blood of Jesus poured out for you and me, and the Holy Spirit came into us to change our hearts. We are now new creations in Christ Jesus—the old has gone, and the new has come (2 Corinthians 5:17).

Because of what Jesus has done for us, we have a destination: we are destined to serve the living God.

> how much more will the blood of Christ, who through the eternal Spirit offered Himself without blemish to God, cleanse your conscience from dead works *to serve the living God*? (Hebrews 9:14)

Keeping all the laws, the rules, the regulations: participating in religion is like investing in dead works. Our destination is not performance but connecting with God. We are cleansed in our conscience so that our hearts can be passionate to serve the living God. Let's not get trapped in dead works. Let's be companions with Christ.

CHAPTER FIFTEEN

THE THREEFOLD ROLE OF JESUS

Hebrews 9:15–28

Some people may believe that all my job as a pastor and preacher entails is coming up with something to say every week. In fact, people will off-handedly joke, "You only work one day a week."

While it is true I have been called to preach and teach the Word of God and be with the members and friends of our church on Sundays, the other five and sometimes six days of the week are filled with a variety of responsibilities. I have to lead the other staff, make sure that the leadership of the ministry areas are growing as teams, mentor developing leaders, counsel people who are struggling and who have special needs, communicate and partner with the elders, make sure I am listening to and learning from others who can speak into my life, work on future sermons and worship services, stay current on reading and on our culture, and spend time in sermon preparation and the planning of services. All of these pastoral roles I must do while staying in connection with the Lord where my relationship with Him is fresh and alive through prayer and personal Bible study.

We all have many roles to play. As we continue in the book of Hebrews, we read this concerning the roles that Jesus plays:

> For this reason He is the mediator of a new covenant, so that, since a death has taken place for the redemption of the transgressions that

129

were committed under the first covenant, those who have been called may receive the promise of the eternal inheritance. (Hebrews 9:15)

Read carefully; this verse seems to be an outline for three roles that Jesus plays. And the rest of Hebrews 9 expands on this verse.

The first role we see Jesus playing is that of "the mediator." "For this reason He is *the mediator* of a new covenant." The original Greek word for "mediator" in this verse is *mesi-tes*. It means "one who reconciles two parties." The word was used often in connection with legal transactions. Like a judge, the opinions or decisions of Jesus are authoritative, for "He *is* the mediator" right now. He is the One who guarantees the certainty of the arrangement, for He is the go-between for us before God the Father.

Through His death He secured the new covenant. This covenant of God is a promise that we will be Christ's companions from now on throughout eternity (as we read back in Hebrews 8:8–12). Look what Hebrews 9:16–17 says:

For where a covenant is, there must of necessity be the death of the one who made it. For a covenant is valid only when men are dead, for it is never in force while the one who made it lives. (Hebrews 9:16–17)

Years ago my wife and I had a will written up. It is a legal document that must be enforced upon our deaths. While we are living, we may change it at any time and it has no authority over anything. Once we die, however, it will have power and meaning. It is the same way with the new covenant: because Jesus died, it is now "in force" and cannot be changed.

Therefore even the first covenant was not inaugurated without blood. For when every commandment had been spoken by Moses to all the people according to the Law, he took the blood of the calves and the goats, with water and scarlet wool and hyssop, and sprinkled both the book itself and all the people, saying, "This is the blood of the covenant which God commanded you." And in the same way he sprinkled both the tabernacle and all the vessels of the ministry with the blood. (Hebrews 9:18–21)

In the Old Testament everything was committed to God by the act of sprinkling the blood of animals. When a priest of the Jewish people[56] acted in faith and took the blood of calves and goats and sprinkled it on the books and the people, it sealed the first covenant, ratifying it and guaranteeing it would be fulfilled. It showed the close relationship between the two parties involved in the covenant. By faith they trusted in what God revealed to them. We are to operate in the same way. By faith we trust in what God has revealed to us today. The new covenant has not been guaranteed by the blood of calves and goats but by the blood of Jesus. He is the mediator, and His blood ratified or sealed our close relationship with God the Father. Jesus has guaranteed our eternal life with God.

So Jesus is the mediator. He is also the liberator. If we go back to Hebrews 9:15, it says:

> For this reason He is the mediator of a new covenant, so that, since *a death has taken place for the redemption of the transgressions that were committed under the first covenant*, those who have been called may receive the promise of the eternal inheritance. (Hebrews 9:15)

In this verse the word "redemption" means to release, to deliver from captivity, or to ransom out of the darkness and bondage of sin. Do you ever wonder why people are pretty content and feel like they are not in bondage or darkness? I read a good illustration that might help us understand why.

John Elliott (1910–1991) was a forest ranger from Alberta, Canada. One winter he was out in a blizzard as he checked for avalanches in the Rocky Mountains. He knew there was a cabin somewhere close and he found it. By the time he got inside to wait out the storm he was somewhat dazed and tired. In his confusion he didn't light a fire or remove his wet clothes. As the blizzard pounded the cabin, wind and snow whistled through the cracks. The soothing sound of the wind sank Elliott into oblivion and he began to doze off. Suddenly, his dog sprang into action. With unrelenting whines he finally managed to rouse his near-comatose friend. The dog was John's constant companion—a St. Bernard. The St. Bernard is a breed famous for their heroics in times like these. Having been woken up by his dog, John started a fire, and weathered the storm. Later he recounted, "If

---

[56] Known as a Levitical priest, or a priest from the descendants of Levi.

my dog hadn't been with me, I'd be dead today. When you are freezing to death you actually feel warm all over, and won't wake up because it feels so good." Today an award is given every year by the Alberta Kennel Club. It is called the John Elliott Perpetual Trophy for St. Bernards.[57]

People are trapped in a spiritual condition where they are out in the wilderness; they are cold toward God. And they are oblivious to the danger they are in. The whistling of the world lulls them into a near-comatose condition. But God is in the business of rousing people from their slumber, helping them realize the trouble they are in. He does this by revealing to them how their sin has a grip on them and that Jesus is near to liberate them.

Jesus is a liberator because His death sealed our forgiveness before God the Father.

> Therefore there is now no condemnation for those who are in Christ Jesus. (Romans 8:1)

> And according to the Law, one may almost say, all things are cleansed with blood, and without shedding of blood there is no forgiveness. (Hebrews 9:22)

In the translation we are using (NASB), the phrase "one may almost say, all things are cleansed with blood" is not the best translation. Almost every other English translation states it better, such as, "under the law almost everything is purified with blood" (ESV). There were only two exceptions under the law where things were not purified with blood: if people were too poor, they could bring flour instead of animals (Leviticus 5:11ff.); and metal objects captured in war could be cleansed by fire and water (Numbers 31:22ff.).

> Therefore it was necessary for the copies of the things in the heavens to be cleansed with these, but the heavenly things themselves with better sacrifices than these. For Christ did not enter a holy place made with hands, a mere copy of the true one, but into heaven itself, now to appear in the presence of God for us; (Hebrews 9:23–24)

---

[57] http://bibleportal.christianpost.com/devotional/inner2.htm?id=8520

Let that sink in. Jesus appears before God our Father "for us"—on our behalf! His nail-scarred hands and feet, the mark of His wound in His side and probably the scars from the crown of thorns are all still present to be a constant reminder that His death sealed our forgiveness.

His death pinpoints the place of power over sin. There was a moment in history when sin lost its power—it was at the cross.

> nor was it that He would offer Himself often, as the high priest enters the holy place year by year with blood that is not his own. Otherwise, He would have needed to suffer often since the foundation of the world; but now once at the consummation of the ages He has been manifested to put away sin by the sacrifice of Himself. (Hebrews 9:25–26)

I love that statement, "at the consummation of the ages." The past, present, and future collided at the cross of Christ. All of sin's power to separate us from God our Father, all of its power to keep us in the dark, all of its power to destroy us was drawn into the place called the Skull,[58] where Jesus hung on the cross. The iniquity of us all was laid on Him.[59] I picture a huge funnel of every offense, every transgression, every deed of darkness from one end of history to the other and the penalty that they deserve poured out on Jesus. It is because of the cross that sin no longer has its hold, its grip, its strength.

Jesus is the mediator, the liberator, and He is the evaluator. He is the One to whom we will have to give an account of our lives. We will stand before Him, and He will make an evaluation.[60] It is the fate of every person that they will die and then face judgment.

> And inasmuch as it is appointed for men to die once and after this comes judgment… (Hebrews 9:27)

I count four judgments the Bible lays out (one of which is

---

[58] Matthew 27:33; Mark 15:22; Luke 23:33; John 19:17.

[59] Isaiah 53:6.

[60] John 5:22, 27; 1 Corinthians 3:10–15.

specifically for Israel).[61] The calling on every Christian's life is to be aware that we will stand before the Lord Jesus and give an account of our lives and that we need to seek an eternal inheritance.

> For this reason He is the mediator of a new covenant, so that, since a death has taken place for the redemption of the transgressions that were committed under the first covenant, *those who have been called may receive the promise of the eternal inheritance.* (Hebrews 9:15)

Notice the author of Hebrews wrote, "May receive." This is a subjunctive verb, which means it is not a guarantee. Every Christian has the possibility to receive an eternal inheritance. Many are saved, but few will inherit or have ownership in eternity;[62] few will be Christ's companions, partners (*metochoi*). This is the central point, the theme, the thesis of the entire book of Hebrews. This eternal ownership goes to those who do what Hebrews 9:28 says:

> so Christ also, having been offered once to bear the sins of many, will appear a second time for salvation without reference to sin, to those who eagerly await Him. (Hebrews 9:28)

A salvation not from the penalty of sin, but a salvation connected to action will be given "to those who eagerly await Him."

Back in May 2011, a man named Harold Camping from Oakland, California, made the news as he declared he had spent decades studying the Bible for coded messages and said, "We know without any shadow of doubt it is going to happen." He was referring to the end of the world, as we know it. He predicted that there would be huge earthquakes, then the rapture, and by October 21, 2011 the

---

[61] (1) The judgment seat of Christ (2 Corinthians 5:10) where Christians, when they are in heaven, will give an account of their lives; (2) the judgment of Israel (Ezekiel 20:33–38) where Old Testament saints and the saved Jewish people from the Tribulation will be judged; (3) the sheep and goats judgment (Matthew 25:31–46) where the nations both saved and unsaved from the Tribulation will be judged at the end of the Tribulation and just before the time of the millennial kingdom; and (4) the great white throne judgment (Revelation 20:11–15) where the mortal people living in the millennial kingdom and the unsaved from history past will be judged.

[62] Matthew 22:1–14 (especially verse 14).

world would be destroyed. The vast majority of Christians are not that radical, but many think to "eagerly await Him" means we get caught up in the signs of the times and constantly evaluate if this is the end.

We know from Hebrews 9 what it means to eagerly await Jesus. It does not mean to be enveloped in reading or listening to the news about the world and trying to understand biblical prophecy and how the two are lining up in order to determine that the end is near. We know from the Bible that the rapture and world events in alignment with prophecy will happen like a thief in the night (1 Thessalonians 5:1–2). The right way to eagerly await the Lord is seen in Hebrews 9:14.

> how much more will the blood of Christ, who through the eternal Spirit offered Himself without blemish to God, cleanse your conscience from dead works to serve the living God? (Hebrews 9:14)

We eagerly await the Lord through working hard at serving the living God. We surrender our lives to be used by Him. We make disciples, teach and admonish each other, spur each other on, reach the lost with the gospel, and build up the saved in Christ.

We all wear many hats both in our personal lives and when we are out in public. We are husbands, wives, sisters, brothers, fathers, mothers, friends, employees, employers, artists, musicians, students, etc. Yet the role that matters most must be played with every hat we wear. No matter what we are doing, we must see ourselves as being companions with Christ. We must honor Him as our liberator and mediator; and we must serve Him now with eager anticipation that what we are doing today is getting ready for the day when we will stand before Him as our evaluator.

CHAPTER SIXTEEN

LIFTING THE BARRIER AND BURDEN OF SIN

Hebrews 10:1–25

I live in Manitowoc, Wisconsin, where one of the largest companies is the Manitowoc Crane Company. They have recently designed a crane, the 31000, with a lifting capacity of 2,535 tons. In tests it lifted 2,750 tons. This means that the 31000 can lift 5.5 million pounds. To get an understanding of how much weight that is, the crane could easily lift over five fully loaded 747 airplanes. Or, if you could devise a way to do so, the 31000 could lift 157 semi-trucks and trailers, each weighing about 35,000 pounds. If you lined them up end to end, the trucks would stretch over two miles long. That crane can lift some serious weight! It took fifty-seven engineers over two years to design it. I find it fascinating that we humans can engineer a machine that can lift that kind of weight. For whatever reason, there was a challenge put before those engineers, and they set their minds and hearts to figuring out how to design a crane capable of lifting that kind of weight.

One of the amazing things about human beings is we are prone to do whatever we set our hearts and minds to do. Whatever it is, if we want it bad enough, we will get it done. But one of our greatest strengths can also be one of our greatest weaknesses. I find it interesting that people think there is a way they can get themselves to

God. The thought is, *If I want it bad enough, I will find a way*. So we repeat a mantra, or face a certain way at certain times of the day and do repetitive prayers, or decide not to do one thing or to do another all with the goal of lifting the barrier between us and God. If we feel like we have done something wrong, we figure out a way to pay some penance or have the good outweigh the bad. If we sense there is a barrier, we think, *Whatever it is, we will find a way; we will try harder.*

I don't enjoy being the bearer of bad news, but I have to level with you: the barrier between God and us is too big for any of us to lift. We can build things that can lift so much, but one thing we cannot lift, no matter how hard we try, is the burden and barrier of our sins. Try as we might, it is impossible to lift it by what we do. If there were ever a guide or a formula, the Bible would spell it out. And, in a sense, it has. In the Bible, God has laid out the law in the Old Testament.[63] A quick summary of the law is found in the Ten Commandments. However, there are over six hundred laws in the Old Testament that govern what you and I could do in order to lift the barrier between God and us. Here's the challenge: "For whoever keeps the whole law and yet stumbles in one point, he has become guilty of all (James 2:10).

As we continue in our study through the book of Hebrews, the first verse of chapter 10 lays out another challenge.

> For the Law, since it has only a shadow of the good things to come and not the very form of things, can never, by the same sacrifices which they offer continually year by year, make perfect those who draw near. (Hebrews 10:1)

It appears from this verse that even keeping the law can never lift the barrier, for the law appears to be "a shadow of the good things to come." In other words, something is still coming in the future. The law spells out what one day we will do naturally. A day is coming when sin will be gone; for God will take it away and those who are Christians will forever live rightly with Him. For now, the barrier and burden of sins cannot be lifted by what we do, no matter how hard we try.

---

[63] In the ancient language of Hebrew, of which the Old Testament is primarily written, the Law is called the Torah, and it is found in the Pentateuch, or the first five books of the Bible.

> Otherwise, would they not have ceased to be offered, because the worshipers, having once been cleansed, would no longer have had consciousness of sins? But in those sacrifices there is a reminder of sins year by year. For it is impossible for the blood of bulls and goats to take away sins. (Hebrews 10:2–4)

I have a bit of a struggle with verse 4. The idea that the blood of bulls and goats could not take away sins seems to contradict what the book of Leviticus lays out. Over fifty times in the book of Leviticus it says that sacrifices were made for the purpose of atonement for the sins of the people. Or, to put it another way, in Leviticus, the blood of bulls and goats was used for the purpose of lifting the barrier and burden of sins in order to reconcile the believers with God. According to Hebrews 10:4, for all those years and all those people, did that mean those sacrifices meant nothing?

Here is how we are to understand it: From the perspective of those Old Testament people (from the human standpoint), they did what they were told to do. They acted in faith. God told them to bring those sacrifices to the tabernacle (and later, to the temple) and offer them up to the Lord, and they did. Because they acted in faith, they entered into God's grace where they experienced His goodness and they were reconciled. However, from God's perspective (from His vantage point) looking at their sins,[64] how they would be cleansed from the guilt of those sins was only by one acceptable sacrifice: the barrier and burden of sins were lifted by what Jesus did.

> Therefore, when He comes into the world, He says, "Sacrifice and offering You have not desired, but a body You have prepared for Me; in whole burnt offerings and sacrifices for sin You have taken no pleasure. Then I said, 'Behold, I have come (in the scroll of the book it is written of Me) to do Your will, O God.'" After saying above, "Sacrifices and offerings and whole burnt offerings and sacrifices for sin You have not desired, nor have You taken pleasure in them" (which are offered according to the Law), then He said, "Behold, I have come to do Your will." He takes away the first in order to establish the second. By this will we have been sanctified through the offering of the body of Jesus Christ once for all. (Hebrews 10:5–10)

---

[64] Not only their sins but ours as well.

As I watched *The Princess Diaries* with my daughters, I thought it a good illustration of the two components of sanctification. Anne Hathaway plays a girl named Mia, who grew up in a single-parent home in San Francisco. As a teenager she finds out that she is actually a princess. Julie Andrews (the queen) first declares to Mia, "You are a princess," then proceeds to help Mia with the guidance she needs to live like a princess. First, it was declared; second, Mia was guided to behave like a princess.

In Hebrews 10:10, "sanctified" means to be made holy, or declared by God to be holy. It is also known in theological circles as being justified (or justification). This is the first component of what it means to be sanctified. The second way people are sanctified is by being in the process of becoming holy. Once we are declared holy, God through His Holy Spirit desires to guide us to learn how and to be empowered to live holy lives. First, we are declared holy; second, we are guided by the Holy Spirit to live holy lives.

> Every priest stands daily ministering and offering time after time the same sacrifices, which can never take away sins; but He, having offered one sacrifice for sins for all time, sat down at the right hand of God, waiting from that time onward until His enemies be made a footstool for His feet. (Hebrews 10:11–13)

The priests always stood, for it was a symbol that their sacred duties were never done (Deuteronomy 18:5). However, after dying on the cross and rising from the dead, Jesus had become the complete offering for our sin. Therefore, He sat down, symbolizing that what He had done to take away the barrier and burden of sin was done. Now He would wait.

Robert E. Lee, commanding general of the Confederate army during the Civil War, straightened his stiff legs, stood high in the stirrups with the big gray horse not moving underneath him. The barren hill all around him sloped down toward the town of Fredericksburg. There was a wide gap of land that the attackers would have to cross in order to engage his soldiers in hand-to-hand combat. Cannons were amassed, and the troops were hunkered down. A clean blanket of snow was on the ground from the night before. It was November 1862. General Lee knew this would be where the next battle would ensue. Although the North had the numbers, Lee had the position. So he waited, and waited…until a month went by. Finally, on December 11, guns began to blast. Shells flew for five days as the town of Fredericksburg became a battleground. That's all it took; in five days the town was reduced to a pile of debris: men dead, buildings smoldering, and one of many battles during those years of the Civil War was over.[65]

Wars come and go, but a constant civil war rages, a spiritual war in the hearts of people. Yes, Jesus sat down, but there are still battles that continue to happen and enemies that still need to be put under His feet. The enemies can be spotted: everything that fights against the Lord Jesus and His saving work. Enemy number one is the devil (Hebrews 2:14). Other enemies connected to the devil are world systems that are not aligned with the Lord's righteousness (Psalm 2); others are people who oppose God and His righteousness (Romans 1:21–32). There are internal wars as well: our sinful nature, our pride, our self-centeredness, our lack of trust, our propensity to sin, etc. We are saved from the penalty of sin, but sin still has its power—it still wages war in our hearts. We can have moments of peace, but it is only a matter of time until the shells of temptation fly and our hearts become a battleground again.

> For by one offering He has perfected for all time those who are sanctified. (Hebrews 10:14)

More accurately, "those who are *being* sanctified." Here the connection between being declared holy and the process of living that way is clearly linked. Just as the queen in *The Princess Diaries* declares that Mia is a princess, then teaches her to behave like one, the one-time action in the past of being declared holy, or having been "perfected for all time" is connected with a continuous impact of learning what that means in the present. "Those who are [being] sanctified" are people who are growing in holiness where the civil-war battles in their lives are being won.

> And the Holy Spirit also testifies to us; for after saying, "This is the covenant that I will make with them after those days, says the Lord: I

---

[65] Adapted from Shaara, *Gods and Generals*, 281–357.

will put My laws upon their heart, and on their mind I will write them,"
He then says, "and their sins and their lawless deeds I will remember no
more." Now where there is forgiveness of these things, there is no longer
any offering for sin. (Hebrews 10:15–18)

This passage may sound familiar. It is almost an exact quote from
Hebrews 8:10–12. It's as if the author puts parentheses around this
section. This wraps up or completes this whole section on the high
priestly ministry of Jesus and how He—and He alone—has lifted the
burden of sin.

Given the fact that Jesus has lifted the barrier and burden of sin,
how should we react? The first thing we'll see as Hebrews 10 continues
is that we ought to draw near to God.

Therefore, brethren, since we have confidence to enter the holy place by
the blood of Jesus, by a new and living way which He inaugurated for us
through the veil, that is, His flesh, and since we have a great priest over
the house of God, let us draw near with a sincere heart in full assurance
of faith, having our hearts sprinkled clean from an evil conscience and
our bodies washed with pure water. (Hebrews 10:19–22)

These verses are like a giant hinge in the book of Hebrews.
The author moves from speaking about Jesus as our high priest to
describing how we might live as His companions. The phrase "washed
with pure water" is not talking about baptism (as some commentators
suggest). Hearing the words "having our hearts sprinkled clean from
an evil conscience and our bodies washed with pure water," the Jewish
Christians who received this book would have known exactly what
the author was referring to. Their minds would've been thinking
about the priests. For before they would come before the Lord in the
tabernacle or temple, the priest had to be sprinkled with blood and
washed with pure water. As Christians, we are cleansed by the blood
of Jesus and washed clean by being born again (or born of the Holy
Spirit). Because of this, like the priests of the Old Testament coming
before the Lord to serve Him, we can draw near to God.

When I was twenty, I made a commitment: I was going to give my
life to drawing near to God. Funny thing, however, when I made that
commitment, it seemed like my life fell apart. My friends at the time
called me a holy roller, and my family thought I was on some kick

(some of them still think this even after two and a half decades). It was a very lonely time in my life, and I thought that all I had was my dog: a dalmatian I named King Solomon (I called him King). At the time, I worked second shift at a hotel, and I was living with a roommate. When I was away, it was not uncommon for my roommate to put King in my room and close the door. One night when I came home, I did as I always did—I went to greet King. When I opened the bedroom door, he gave me one of those looks. His ears were down, his tail was down, his head was lowered, and he gave me those puppy-dog eyes even though he was a full-grown adult. Clearly he had done something wrong that he didn't want me to find out about. It didn't take me long to realize that King had found my Bible and had completely shredded it. It was like confetti spread all over my bed and on the floor. I'm not exaggerating when I say there was not a single piece of my Bible that was larger than two inches in diameter. I had committed myself to Jesus, and it felt as if my friends had forsaken me, my family had forsaken me, and now even King (*man's best friend*) had forsaken me.

Even when we feel alone in this world, Jesus is always near. Nothing can stand between Him and us, and He will never leave us, nor forsake us (Hebrews 13:5); for He is always faithful. No matter what happens in our lives, because Jesus has lifted the barrier and burden of our sins, we can draw near with a sincere heart in full assurance of our faith. Therefore, no matter what is happening in our lives,

> let us hold fast the confession of our hope without wavering, for He who promised is faithful; (Hebrews 10:23)

I've noticed that many Christians nowadays seem to be mixing and matching God's truth with whatever they feel is their own truth. It seems as if the truth of God is being watered down. For instance, not too long ago a young woman gave her life to Christ and said she wanted to follow the Lord. Then she started dating a young man who did not share the same values. Instead of seeking the Lord's will on appropriate boundaries, she decided to set her own boundaries.

Another example was a young couple who had a newborn baby. They came from a tradition that said babies were to be baptized in case they died in infancy. Their tradition taught that water baptisms would cover the babies until they could make a choice for or against Jesus.

After talking to them about what the Bible says on water baptism and the grace of God as it relates to small children, their conclusion was to get their baby baptized anyway, saying, "Better safe than sorry."

Many Christian couples who are considering divorce will often conclude, *God just wants me to be happy, right?* The list can go on and on with Christians who are not completely committed to seeking out and clinging to God's truth. It is our duty to set people on the path of truth. Nowadays it appears that people are becoming biblically illiterate. We are just one generation away from people believing lies instead of God's absolute truth.[66] The church is to be the pillar and foundation of the truth (1 Timothy 3:15). If we don't cling to it and proclaim it, who will?

I realize it is difficult to cling to the truth in our modern age. Therefore, we must continue to encourage each other.

> and let us consider how to stimulate one another to love and good deeds, not forsaking our own assembling together, as is the habit of some, but encouraging one another; and all the more as you see the day drawing near. (Hebrews 10:24–25)

That last phrase, "as you see the day drawing near," has caused many people to offer different opinions or speculations as to what that "day" is. Given the theme of the whole book of Hebrews—to be companions or partners with Jesus now and forever—we know this life matters for eternity. The "day" in the context of the whole book of Hebrews is speaking of that day when, in a twinkling of an eye, in an instant, we will go to be with the Lord (1 Corinthians 15:52). That day is drawing near! So we must encourage one another all the more!

In Hebrews 10:22, 23, and 24, with every exhortation these words were used: "let us." We are in this together—we have to be. We cannot draw near or cling to the truth or even spur each other on toward love and good deeds on our own. God made us to live in community in order to learn and grow in what it means to love Him and love each other.

Life has its highs and lows. It can be challenging and even weigh

---

[66] As in the days of the Judges when the Israelites had no king and everyone did what was right in their own eyes (Judges 17:6; 21:25).

heavy upon us. Even though Jesus lifted the barrier and burden of sins, which placed us in a position before God as being declared holy, the battles still rage. There are external wars where the world around us tries to pull us away from the Lord. There are internal wars where we still have to fight our old nature. We need each other—we do! And all the more as we see what is going on around us; and all the more as we see that Jesus will come back soon, maybe even today.

So let us encourage each other, stir each other up, stimulate each other's thinking, challenge each other on how we are living, and spur each other on toward love and good deeds. Together, *let us* draw near to God and we will see His power lifting something weightier than anything a Manitowoc Crane 31000 could ever lift. First, He lifts the penalty of sin and puts us in a position of being sanctified (also known as justification). Then, if we let Him, He will lift the weight of the power that sin has over our lives and grow us in the process of sanctification. When we see growth happening in each other's lives, we will say together, "Jesus is the victor! Jesus is our Savior!"

PART IV

LIVING IN THE LIGHT OF ETERNITY

Hebrews 10:26–13:25

CHAPTER SEVENTEEN

IT IS RIGHT

Hebrews 10:26–39

Robert Fulghum wrote a book that was first published in 1988 titled *All I Really Need to Know I Learned in Kindergarten*. It is a lighthearted yet profound book on how to live wisely. Things such as play fair, don't hit people, clean up your own mess, say you're sorry when you hurt somebody, wash your hands before you eat, and take a nap every afternoon are just a few of the suggestions in the book. Those kinds of tips are words to live by. If we all did those things, the world would be a better place. You know why? Because they are the right things to do.

It seems somewhat natural to know what the right things to do are (even though we don't always do them). Yet I think the lines get blurred when some things that we assume are right are actually wrong. For instance, "The end justifies the means," "It's okay to holler at someone if they deserve it," "Lying is okay in some circumstances," or, "Sometimes it's right to turn a blind eye to sin." When it comes to our Christianity, for the most part I think we know what is right. Yet our concept of right and wrong can become unclear. We can paint a picture of what our relationship with the Lord is all about, but our picture can get distorted and our expectations can become skewed.

The entire book of Hebrews is about what it takes to be companions or partners with Christ both now and forever. The author of the book will now head full-steam through the end of the letter by talking about living our lives focused on eternity. He will start by giving us an understanding of what is right in our relationship with God. These truths may be things that go contrary to what we've always believed, or maybe we have never thought about them before. This next section may stretch us a bit—if we let it.

It is not uncommon for us to view God as a big, soft, lovable, gentle, kind, compassionate, tender Father who is all-powerful but who rarely, if ever, exerts His power (at least not in our experience). In many respects, all of that is true. Yet we would be making a huge mistake if we think that we have nothing to fear with God, because we do. It is right to have a healthy fear of God. Look at these sobering words that come next in the book of Hebrews:

> For if we go on sinning willfully after receiving the knowledge of the truth, there no longer remains a sacrifice for sins, but a terrifying expectation of judgment and the fury of a fire which will consume the adversaries. (Hebrews 10:26–27)

This is addressed to Christians. Notice the personal pronoun "we." The author includes himself in this warning. The Christians this passage addresses are those of us who deliberately do what is wrong when we have been shown what God's will is. The author has just said that we have to continue meeting together and encouraging each other (Hebrews 10:24–25). And in Hebrews 3:12–13, we are told to encourage each other daily so that we are not hardened by the deceitfulness of sin. Hebrews 5:11–12 instructs us not to become dull of hearing. Later, we are warned not to fall away from the Lord (Hebrews 6:1–8), and we are told not to drift away (Hebrews 2:1). Even though God's way is the right way, Christians can willingly turn their backs on the Lord and refuse to live life the way He desires us to live.

Let's look again at what the author says in Hebrews 10:26:

> For if we go on sinning willfully after receiving the knowledge of the truth, there no longer remains a sacrifice for sins, (Hebrews 10:26)

Remember the original audience? These were Christians who came out of Judaism. I picture them having the mentality of *I can go on sinning because I can bring an animal to the temple tomorrow and have it sacrificed and everything will be fine.* In our time we don't bring animals to be sacrificed, but we do bring our sacrifices, metaphorically speaking. We've adapted our sacrifices to our times; we say, "I'll just confess tomorrow," or, "I'm in church, aren't I? That's got to count for something," or, "I'm not as bad as some others." It's as if we bring our sacrifices for our sins over and over and in some way justify our misbehavior. This is even after we've been enlightened by what the Lord desires of us.

Jesus died for our sins once and for all. When we trust Him, we cross over from death to life (John 5:24), from being orphans to being children of God (John 1:12). Our eternal life is settled: We will be with the Lord forever. However, if we go on willfully sinning, there is something very serious we must fear:

> but a terrifying expectation of judgment and the fury of a fire which will consume the adversaries. (Hebrews 10:27)

This is the fourth of five warnings that Hebrews directs to Christians. It is not speaking of hell, but the author uses a picture of fire to describe God's anger. It is an anger similar to that He will have against His adversaries. The warning to us is that we should never patronize God. You may have heard people say, "Don't patronize me!" which means, "Don't act like you are superior to me and I don't really matter to you." A synonym listed for patronize in Merriam-Webster is "lord (it over)."[67] It is similar to people who say they are committed to the Lord without *really* being committed to Him, as if the Lord is truthfully below them and He really doesn't matter to them.

> Anyone who has set aside the Law of Moses dies without mercy on the testimony of two or three witnesses. How much severer punishment do you think he will deserve who has trampled under foot the Son of God, and has regarded as unclean the blood of the covenant by which he was sanctified, and has insulted the Spirit of grace? (Hebrews 10:28–29)

Notice again this is talking about a Christian: "by which he was sanctified." We are not superior to God. He doesn't cater to us; we are

---

[67] http://merriam-webster.com/dictionary/patronize.

called to cater to Him. It is possible for Christians to "insult" the Spirit of grace. The word "insulted" (*enybri'zo*) means to have an excessive self-confidence, or such an arrogance that leads to mistreating or scoffing at something or someone to the point of insulting another. In this case, insulting God and His grace.

In 1969, in Pass Christian, Mississippi, a group of people in an upscale apartment were having a "hurricane party." Hurricane Camille was heading straight for that small town. Police Chief Jerry Peralta knocked on their door in order to warn them of the danger. The owner of the building scoffed at Chief Peralta and said, "This is my land; if you want me off, you'll have to arrest me." Chief Peralta did not arrest them, but he asked if he could take down their names in case there were any people they needed to look for after the hurricane hit. At 10:15 p.m., the storm hit. By the time it was over, winds in excess of 205 mph had been recorded—the strongest winds ever on record from a hurricane. To give you some comparison: a category 5 (the worst category) maintains winds of 155 mph. Hurricane Camille brought rain that hit buildings like bullets and waves up to twenty-eight feet high that pummeled the shores of the Gulf of Mexico. By the time it was over, twenty people had died in Pass Christian...all of them from that apartment. Nothing was left but the foundation. The only survivor from the apartment was a five-year-old boy who was clinging to a mattress.[68]

There is a hurricane coming, and the warning has been given that God will not tolerate a patronizing attitude.

> For we know Him who said, "Vengeance is Mine, I will repay." And again, "The Lord will judge His people." It is a terrifying thing to fall into the hands of the living God. (Hebrews 10:30–31)

God's punishment—His vengeance and justice—will be carried out. He will do it either in this life as He disciplines His children (Hebrews 12) or in the future when we stand before His judgment seat in heaven (1 Corinthians 3:10–15; 2 Corinthians 5:10). He will not carry out what Hebrews 10:30–31 says by casting His children (Christians) into

---

[68] Adapted from "Arrogance," Sermon Illustrations, accessed January 19, 2014, www.sermonillustrations.com/a-z/a/arrogance.htm.

hell. But for those Christians who do not have a healthy fear of God, He will clearly bring His vengeance and judgment. This judgment will bring Christians who have gone on willfully sinning in their lives on earth to the point where they will be weeping and gnashing their teeth (Matthew 8:12;[69] 22:13; 24:51; 25:30; Luke 13:28). Doing the right thing, living according to God's will, is not always easy. But when we grow to know what is right, calling on the Lord to help us, we have to obey it. It's that simple.

It is also right to endure in our faith for God's sake, even when it hurts. When I was nineteen years old, a couple of my friends dared me to hop on a train that was moving pretty slowly. At that time in my life, if I was given a dare, I typically took it. So I ran alongside the train and jumped on one of the cars. The train quickly gained speed, and I thought, *I have to work tomorrow.* My very next thought was, *How can I get off this train?* The only option I could see was I had to jump. On one side of the train car was a steep gully; on the other side was another set of tracks and then a flat field. I decided to try to jump over the second set of tracks with the hope of landing in the field. Now, by this time the train was traveling at speeds that you couldn't keep up with even if you were on a fifteen-speed bicycle pedaling as fast as you could. So I stood on the side of the train car, and with all my might I leaped out as far as I could. I went soaring through the air and...didn't quite make it over the second set of tracks. I smacked pretty hard on the cold, hard steel of the rail and ended up having to go to the hospital to get some stitches. My head hurt for many days afterward, and I decided I would never jump on—or off—a train again as long as I lived, because it hurt too much.

It is human nature to avoid pain. The last thing I wanted was to get hurt, and upon getting hurt, I vowed I would never put myself in that situation again. What's interesting is God sometimes calls us to do what is contrary to our natural tendencies. At times He calls us to head into pain, to head into trials, to try not to sidestep or avoid them. What the author of Hebrews says next is we must be willing to suffer at times.

---

[69] To be clear on who the "sons of the kingdom" are, go to the only other place in Matthew where that phrase is used: Matthew 13:38.

But remember the former days, when, after being enlightened, you endured a great conflict of sufferings, partly by being made a public spectacle through reproaches and tribulations, and partly by becoming sharers with those who were so treated. For you showed sympathy to the prisoners and accepted joyfully the seizure of your property, knowing that you have for yourselves a better possession and a lasting one. (Hebrews 10:32–34)

Clearly the first recipients of this letter went through some major suffering, mistreatment, and pain. It reminds me of the words of Jesus recorded in Revelation 2:8–10:

And to the angel of the church in Smyrna write: The first and the last, who was dead, and has come to life, says this: "I know your tribulation and your poverty (but you are rich), and the blasphemy by those who say they are Jews and are not, but are a synagogue of Satan. Do not fear what you are about to suffer. Behold, the devil is about to cast some of you into prison, so that you will be tested, and you will have tribulation for ten days. Be faithful until death, and I will give you the crown of life." (Revelation 2:8–10)

How would you like to get that news? What Jesus was saying was, "Here's the deal: you're going to suffer, but I want you to endure through it because in ten days you'll be put to death. That's the bad news. Here's the good news: you will be rewarded afterward with the crown of life" (see James 1:12). The author of Hebrews challenges us today to be willing to suffer for God. Are we willing to give up all we possess for possessions that will last for eternity—eternal rewards like the crown of life?

Life can get tough and uncomfortable: marriages can feel like they are crumbling; our jobs can feel uncertain; our finances can be tight; we can even experience people mocking us because of our faith. It is human nature to try to get out from underneath those things in order to avoid the pain. But that may not be God's will. God wants us to have our hearts set on Him, faithfully serving Him in the good times and in the bad.

Therefore, do not throw away your confidence, which has a great reward. For you have need of endurance, so that when you have done the will of God, you may receive what was promised. (Hebrews 10:35–36)

The author of Hebrews here seems to be telling us if we endure and don't willfully turn our backs on God and His will, we will be rewarded.

Recently I had a conversation with a friend who was going through a marital struggle. I reminded him about the covenant or vow he made before God on his wedding day and how those vows matter most when things are going badly. At the time I thought (I didn't say it, although looking back I wish I would have), *Even if the rest of your life your marriage is a struggle, do the will of God—seek to please Him.* The marriage was uncomfortable and how he and his wife were treating each other wasn't right. I longed for them both to seek to do God's will! Because this passage was on my mind during our discussion, I thought, *Be willing to endure suffering; God will reward you.*

What is most important for us, if we are going to endure in our Christian walk, is trust.

> For yet in a very little while, he who is coming will come, and will not delay. But My righteous one shall live by faith; and if he shrinks back, My soul has no pleasure in him. But we are not of those who shrink back to destruction, but of those who have faith to the preserving of the soul. (Hebrews 10:37–39)

The way to keep our soul (in this context it means "life") from God's vengeance, anger, and judgment is by walking by faith. God wants the very best for us—He really does! That's why He is so serious about sin. Sin is like a sickness, and God wants us to get better. He wants us to endure even through the hard times, because He wants our very best now and for eternity. Living by faith is submitting to Him, following Him, and completely trusting Him, even when life hurts. It means that we believe that God loves us and brings us through trials not only to grow us now but so we may receive what was promised in the future. God loves us, and when we walk by faith, it is as if we are saying to Him, "I love You back."

CHAPTER EIGHTEEN

A FAITH THAT IS FIT

Hebrews 11:1–40

As Christians, we place our faith in Jesus that one day we will be with Him in heaven and ultimately spend eternity with Him. As we have learned, the book of Hebrews is all about being with Jesus as His companion or partner now and ultimately in the eternity to come. Until that day we are to live by faith. Yet in the last chapter (specifically Hebrews 10:38–39) we read it is clear some Christians have a faith that is weak or feeble— literally a faith that shrinks back. So how do we keep our faith healthy and strong? How do we endure, staying filled up in our faith; how do we persevere in our faith?

The title of this chapter is "A Faith That Is Fit." With all the things that can break us down from having a healthy faith (from temptations to being too tired, from wanting to be in control to having our lives spin out of control), how do we have a faith the Lord would find a pleasure to observe in us? How can we maintain a faith that is fit? Hebrews 11 was written to answer just that.

The chapter begins by giving us a definition of *faith* so that we can zoom in on a clear understanding of what we're talking about when it comes to our faith as Christians or followers of Jesus.

> Now faith is the assurance of things hoped for, the conviction of things not seen. For by it the men of old gained approval. (Hebrews 11:1–2)

Have you ever hoped for something, where you just knew it was going to happen, only to have hope begin to slip through your fingers like sand? In our lives this is very common. It starts when we are young. Children hope for a present at Christmas they don't receive, or they hope for a teacher they don't get. As we get older, the ability to hope continues to be attacked. We hope for a job and do not get it, or we hope for a spouse and remain single. We hope our marriage improves, or we hope for children, or we hope that our children turn out okay... Over and over again our hopes and dreams seem to be erased by reality. But God and His Word tell us, "Don't give up on hoping. Don't give up on believing. Keep your inner conviction of the things that are not seen."

Even though the unseen future will one day be real, today we can only trust in what we hope for. Although we place our faith or our confidence and inner conviction in what is not seen, one way to hope is to hear the testimony of others and see the testimony of the historical record that the Bible holds. Looking over our shoulder at the past has a profound power to strengthen our faith in the present. This is what the author of Hebrews did: He asked the original recipients of this letter to look over their shoulders. He called them to look way back—all the way to the beginning—and gave three examples of having a faith that is fit.

> By faith we understand that the worlds were prepared by the word of God, so that what is seen was not made out of things which are visible. By faith Abel offered to God a better sacrifice than Cain, through which he obtained the testimony that he was righteous, God testifying about his gifts, and through faith, though he is dead, he still speaks. By faith Enoch was taken up so that he would not see death; and he was not found because God took him up; for he obtained the witness that before his being taken up he was pleasing to God. (Hebrews 11:3–5)

A faith that is fit is a faith that is focused. Our faith must be focused on something. As Christians, we don't believe in just a concept, we believe in a supreme being. We don't believe in a higher power (like "the Force" in Star Wars), we believe in the one true God. Therefore, a faith that is fit is a faith that is focused on God.

And without faith it is impossible to please Him, for he who comes to God must believe that He is… (Hebrews 11:6a)

Doing great things for God, giving our riches to the things of the Lord, being involved in ministry, etc., all mean nothing unless these things are done from a heart of faith, where we believe, first of all, that God *is*.

In Exodus 3, Moses was a shepherd of sheep for his father-in-law, Jethro. One day, while on Mount Sinai, God called him to lead the Israelites out of Egypt. Moses lacked hope. He didn't think the people would follow him. So he asked God, "Now they may say to me, 'What is His name?' What shall I say to them?" God replied, "I Am Who I Am" (in Hebrew it was all one word, "Yahweh"). God went on to instruct Moses to tell his people, "I Am has sent me to you." Believing in God, Moses went to free God's people from their slavery in Egypt.

In John 8, Jesus was interacting with the Jewish leaders in the temple. The Jews said to him, "Surely You are not greater than our father Abraham, who died?" Jesus said, "Your father Abraham rejoiced to see My day." Jesus was indicating that He had some kind of a relationship with Abraham; so the religious leaders replied, "You are not yet fifty years old, and have You seen Abraham?" Jesus said, "Truly, truly, I say to you, before Abraham was born, I am." The Jewish religious leaders knew that Jesus was saying He was God. So they picked up stones to throw at Him because claiming to be God was an offense worthy of death. But Jesus was able to slip out of the temple unharmed.

Jesus declared Himself to be "I Am." God declared himself to be "I Am Who I Am." God is! If our faith is going to be fit, we must believe that God is—that He is real. If "God is," then it only makes sense that we respond to Him as God. Therefore, we submit to Him, we live for Him, we seek His truth in the Bible. When we learned it, we trust in Him because He is. And then we believe He will reward us if we seek Him.

And without faith it is impossible to please Him, for he who comes to God must believe that He is and that He is a rewarder of those who seek Him. (Hebrews 11:6)

Notice both the words "comes" and "seek." Both of these verbs are present participles, which means they are continuous actions in the present. It may be more accurate to say "is coming," and "are seeking." This isn't something that happened one time somewhere back in the past; this is a walk of faith. This is where we pursue Him, where we are approaching Him consistently. It means we are inquiring, learning, growing, and investing in our relationship with Him.

A world-class female runner was invited to compete in a road race in Connecticut. On the morning of the race she drove her Mazda Miata from New York to the place where she thought the race was being held. She had gotten the directions months before, over the phone, which she had written down on a piece of paper. However, she seemed to be lost. She pulled into a gas station and asked the attendant if he knew of a road race somewhere nearby. He did recall that there was a race not too far down the street. She drove the short distance, and upon arriving, she realized there were not as many runners as she had anticipated. One of her first thoughts was that this race was going to be easier than she had expected. When she came to the table for her registration, the officials recognized her and were excited that this renowned runner was going to run in their race. They could not find her registration but quickly signed her up before the starting gun would go off. She did such a spectacular job in the race that she ended up four minutes ahead of the second-place runner (who happened to be the first-place male runner). After the race, she was a bit confused that she didn't receive any prize money. But then things started adding up for her. She realized the race she was invited to was not the race she had just competed in. She had gone to the wrong starting line, ran the wrong course, and missed her chance to win the valuable reward.

We are all running a race, but are we at the right starting line? Are we running the right course? We don't want to miss out on our chance to win the valuable rewards God has for us. The race God calls us to run is to endure in seeking Him. And if we run this race well, there will be a reward for us in the future. The author of Hebrews used both Noah and Abraham to illustrate this point.

By faith Noah, being warned by God about things not yet seen, in reverence prepared an ark for the salvation of his household, by which he condemned the world, and became an heir of the righteousness which is according to faith. By faith Abraham, when he was called, obeyed by going out to a place which he was to receive for an inheritance; and he went out, not knowing where he was going. By faith he lived as an alien in the land of promise, as in a foreign land, dwelling in tents with Isaac and Jacob, fellow heirs of the same promise; for he was looking for the city which has foundations, whose architect and builder is God. By faith even Sarah herself received ability to conceive, even beyond the proper time of life, since she considered Him faithful who had promised. Therefore there was born even of one man, and him as good as dead at that, as many descendants as the stars of heaven in number, and innumerable as the sand which is by the seashore. All these died in faith, without receiving the promises, but having seen them and having welcomed them from a distance, and having confessed that they were strangers and exiles on the earth. For those who say such things make it clear that they are seeking a country of their own. And indeed if they had been thinking of that country from which they went out, they would have had opportunity to return. But as it is, they desire a better country, that is, a heavenly one. Therefore God is not ashamed to be called their God; for He has prepared a city for them. (Hebrews 11:7–16)

They didn't look back. They decided to leave their past—their place of comfort—and fully commit themselves to following the Lord. Because they had an assurance of things hoped for, they believed in a place that God was making where they would live with Him forever. They had a deep conviction of things that are not yet seen. Do we? Where do we place our faith?

By faith Abraham, when he was tested, offered up Isaac, and he who had received the promises was offering up his only begotten son; it was he to whom it was said, "In Isaac your descendants shall be called." He considered that God is able to raise people even from the dead, from which he also received him back as a type. By faith Isaac blessed Jacob and Esau, even regarding things to come. By faith Jacob, as he was dying, blessed each of the sons of Joseph, and worshiped, leaning on the top of his staff. By faith Joseph, when he was dying, made mention of the exodus of the sons of Israel, and gave orders concerning his bones. (Hebrews 11:17–22)

Abraham believed in the resurrection. Do we? Believing in the resurrection ought to give us hope. For every follower of the Lord who has ever lived must understand and believe this truth: because Jesus Christ was resurrected, we will experience the resurrection. There will come a time when we will be given new and eternal physical bodies. If we seek the Lord now, we can be sure, because of the resurrection, God will reward us for seeking Him.

Here's another twist to this truth we can put our faith in: God will reward those who seek Him…and He will do it now (in others words, in this life). The author of Hebrews now gives examples of how God has rewarded people even in their lives before they died.

> By faith Moses, when he was born, was hidden for three months by his parents, because they saw he was a beautiful child; and they were not afraid of the king's edict. By faith Moses, when he had grown up, refused to be called the son of Pharaoh's daughter, choosing rather to endure ill-treatment with the people of God than to enjoy the passing pleasures of sin, considering the reproach of Christ greater riches than the treasures of Egypt; for he was looking to the reward. By faith he left Egypt, not fearing the wrath of the king; for he endured, as seeing Him who is unseen. By faith he kept the Passover and the sprinkling of the blood, so that he who destroyed the firstborn would not touch them. By faith they passed through the Red Sea as though they were passing through dry land; and the Egyptians, when they attempted it, were drowned. By faith the walls of Jericho fell down after they had been encircled for seven days. By faith Rahab the harlot did not perish along with those who were disobedient, after she had welcomed the spies in peace. And what more shall I say? For time will fail me if I tell of Gideon, Barak, Samson, Jephthah, of David and Samuel and the prophets, who by faith conquered kingdoms, performed acts of righteousness, obtained promises, shut the mouths of lions, quenched the power of fire, escaped the edge of the sword, from weakness were made strong, became mighty in war, put foreign armies to flight. Women received back their dead by resurrection; (Hebrews 11:23–35a)

Everything was moving up and to the right! People were trusting God, and He was providing in miraculous ways! This almost seems like a "name it, claim it" gospel. That is a term that describes hope in the Lord this way: if you have enough faith, you will see God doing amazing things. The truth is, living a life of faith, we may see God do just that. We may see God do incredible things in our lives today. We may experience His reward in our lives even now. However, before we jump to the conclusion that having a faith that is fit will *always* result in seeing God's reward now, let's continue reading:

> and others were tortured, not accepting their release, so that they might obtain a better resurrection; and others experienced mockings and scourgings, yes, also chains and imprisonment. They were stoned, they were sawn in two, they were tempted, they were put to death with the sword; they went about in sheepskins, in goatskins, being destitute, afflicted, ill-treated (men of whom the world was not worthy), wandering in deserts and mountains and caves and holes in the ground. (Hebrews 11:35–38)

A faith that is fit trusts in the Lord even when we don't see positive results. Years ago, as I was leading a men's Bible study that met early in the morning on Tuesdays, a young man was invited to attend. Shortly after he started, he realized that he was not a Christian. We shared the gospel with him, and he received Jesus as his Savior and was very joy filled. The rest of the men in the group, me included, were overjoyed also. As this young man got to know us, he began to share some deep wounds from his past. The men in the group were very supportive. Then, out of the blue, he stopped coming. It was as if he just fell off the map. I finally tracked him down and asked him why he stopped coming. He said, "God didn't take away my pain. Nothing is different." Sadly, his focus was on himself and he treated God like a pain pill. God to him was only there to soothe his pain, not to be his strength in the midst of the pain.

He wasn't the first person to have this view, nor will he be the last. When we hear amazing stories from Christians and how God has done such radical things in their lives, we think that is the norm. The truth is, historically, many Christians don't see God's mighty hand working in this life. They experience pain and suffering, and they can never get away from it. God does not seem to rescue them from those circumstances. There is no good way to answer the deep problem of pain without a deep hope and faith in God and His eternity. A faith that is fit is a faith not focused on our present circumstances, but a faith that is focused on being with God one day and looking forward to forever with Him.

> And all these, having gained approval through their faith, did not receive

what was promised, because God had provided something better for us, so that apart from us they would not be made perfect. (Hebrews 11:39–40)

There was a solid Christian man in our church who owned a sailboat. Sailing was one of the things he loved to do. Unfortunately he had a rare cancer caused by mesothelioma (an asbestos-related cancer) that took his life. A day after he died, I was talking to his wife, who was acutely aware of the truth that God will reward those who seek Him. She asked me a deep and meaningful question that was very intense given the fact that her husband had been with Jesus for about twenty-four hours at the time. She asked, "Has David [her husband] stood before Jesus already where he has been rewarded for his faithfully following Him? Has he been put in charge of anything yet?" And then she smiled and added, "Because if he has, he's probably in charge of a shipyard somewhere in the corner of heaven because of how much he loved sailing."

I had to jog my memory and think back on some timelines that I had drawn up years ago for some of my seminary classes, trying to remember when these eternal rewards will be handed out. These verses (Hebrews 11:39–40) seem to indicate an event will happen in the future, after the resurrection, where we will be made perfect—where our eternal state will be established. It seems like we will be together before the throne of Jesus and He will reward us and we will receive what He has promised at that time. In the resurrection our eternal bodies will replace our heavenly bodies; then we will be given cities, countries, continents to live in and take responsibility for. And what will determine our responsibility then (according to Hebrews 11:39) is how we gain that approval now. And the only way to please God is by faith—a faith that is fit! The only faith that is fit is a faith that has hope—a hope in the future because we believe that God is and that He is a rewarder of those who seek Him.

Chapter Nineteen

RUN WITH ENDURANCE

Hebrews 12:1–17

A few years ago I gave up a dream: to be a runner for the rest of my life, to compete in road races, and even to run marathons into old age. At forty I had surgery on my left knee. I knew if I kept running, my knees would not be able to take the pounding over the years to come. I determined I had to take up a new form of aerobic exercise, so I switched to biking. I still love to watch competitions like track and field in the Olympics and marathons that take place around our world. One of the most fascinating is held in London. It is unique because of those who participate. Actually, not so much the runners themselves, but the costumes they wear. It is one thing to be able to run 26.2 miles; it's quite another to do so dressed up like a camel, a huge doll, a soccer player who bobbles a ball on his foot the entire way, or a knight pulling a dragon. That is the nature of the London Marathon. None of the runners who dress up in costumes ever win the race or even compete for top spots, but it is so entertaining to see them make their way along in their creative garb.

Running is one of America's favorite pastimes. If we want to communicate to the world around us that we are staying in shape, running is one of the main ways we do it. Actually, because we are Christians, God sees all of us as runners in a race. We are not running against each other to overtake or defeat one another. The goal is to persevere until the end—to run well and cross the finish line. The reality is, like some runners in marathons, many Christians stop running spiritually. In the race we are in, we must keep a steady pace and run to win the prize. The book of Hebrews lays out what that prize is: *being companions with Christ right now and throughout eternity.*

In the race, the course we are to run has been set, and we are called to run it well.

> Therefore, since we have so great a cloud of witnesses surrounding us, let us also lay aside every encumbrance and the sin which so easily entangles us, and let us run with endurance the race that is set before us... (Hebrews 12:1)

I have read about the awareness of "run[ning] with endurance" that those first recipients of this letter may have had. The Greeks influenced the Romans' belief that true education included physical exercise. Sport became such a part of the culture they actually regulated it by laws. From the age of seven into adulthood everyone had to exercise. The Romans built gymnasiums and stadiums for competition. The academies emphasized not just mental training but bodily training as well. By the time the author wrote Hebrews, athletic games were held in most Roman provinces. The people of the New Testament era knew the difference between a sprint and a long-distance run. The message written in Hebrews likened the life of a Christian to a long-distance run.

What is peculiar about this run is seen at the end of verse 1, "the race that is set before us." God has set our course; we get to decide if we are going to stay on it or not. God has a desired path for us, and the course is not easy to run. But just like a marathon, the race can be exhilarating. God wants to encourage us to keep pressing on. That is why, after listing all the people who have gone before us living faithfully for the Lord (as we just saw in Hebrews 11), the author gives this encouraging exhortation in Hebrews 12:1, as if to say, "If they can do it, you can do it too! All it takes is being committed."

> Therefore, since we have so great a cloud of witnesses surrounding us, *let us also lay aside every encumbrance and the sin which so easily entangles us,* and let us run with endurance the race that is set before us, (Hebrews 12:1)

In the London Marathon, the winners every year are not those wearing costumes. They are the runners who wear the bare minimum: lightweight shirts, shorts, and shoes. To run this race of following Jesus by faith, we have to be committed to winning. The only way to win is by laying aside those things that encumber us (like those bulky costumes on most of the London Marathon runners) and the sin that entangles us. So many things can drag on us. We can identify sin pretty easily, but what are encumbrances? To answer that, we must ask ourselves the question "What is it that takes most of our attention?" For many people, they may say something like, "Our kids," or, "My job," or, "A hobby," etc. When we think about what takes most of our attention, does the name of Jesus come to mind? If not, we have an encumbrance—something bulky that needs to be laid aside; not forgotten, just moved down a shelf or two. What needs to be on the primary shelf in our hearts and in our minds—at eye level—is in the next verse:

> fixing our eyes on Jesus, the author and perfecter of faith, who for the joy set before Him endured the cross, despising the shame, and has sat down at the right hand of the throne of God. (Hebrews 12:2)

When running, it is always best to keep looking at the horizon and not stare down at the ground just in front of our feet. It is not easy to fix our eyes on Jesus. What makes it difficult is He is not as tangible as the ground at our feet, or as the struggles that are right in front of us. Jesus may not seem as real as the challenges of our jobs, what our kids are dealing with, or any number of things that are happening in our lives. Often, this is what we do: when we are struggling, we fix our eyes on our struggle and if Jesus can help, great! But that focus is wrong. Jesus is not like a genie in a bottle where we call on Him only to help fix things. We need Jesus more than we need our marriages to be healed, our finances to be in a better place, friends to hang out with, or our lives to be fixed in some way. When we are helping people, remember what they need most—they need Jesus! We need to place our full trust in Jesus, who is the author and perfecter of our faith.

> For consider Him who has endured such hostility by sinners against Himself, so that you will not grow weary and lose heart. You have not

yet resisted to the point of shedding blood in your striving against sin; (Hebrews 12:3–4)

The word "consider" (verse 3), in the original language, appears only here in the Bible. This word is an imperative, which means it is a command. To capture the essence of this verb, we would demand, "Be thinking about Jesus." When our course gets tough, we may want to drop out of the race. What these verses tell us is to endure and stay thinking about Jesus.

Not only is the course set, but also the coach is set. God has established Himself as our Father—this is true. Our Father trains us. He coaches us, and we must follow Him. Just like anyone who is in training, we must expect discipline.

and you have forgotten the exhortation which is addressed to you as sons, "My son, do not regard lightly the discipline of the Lord, nor faint when you are reproved by Him; for those whom the Lord loves He disciplines, and He scourges every son whom He receives." (Hebrews 12:5–6)

Verse 5 starts out with "and you have forgotten." We may wonder why God would allow tough times, challenges, or struggles to come our way. We may think, *Doesn't He love us?* as if we have forgotten how He loves us. The truth is, a good parent or coach wants his or her charge to encounter times of uneasiness and challenge. These verses say, "Do not forget what God our loving Father is doing."

The only way to grow us is to stretch us. God does this in three ways. First, the word "discipline" (*paideia* in the original language of Greek) literally means "child training." God trains us by guidance given to develop us to live responsibly for Him. Second, God may 'reprove' us (verse 5). That means God will shed light on the junk in our lives He wants to work on. Sometimes, God will use a third level. When, like weeds in a garden, we hold to deeply rooted unrighteousness, God knows only "scourges" can drive it out (verse 6; see also Proverbs 22:15). This *scourging* can look like God bringing us through some difficult situations in life. He does this to yank out that unholy stuff and smooth away our rough edges.

Growing up, I got spankings. I probably needed them. My parents tried to instill in me a sense of responsibility for things. One task they gave me was to take care of our chickens. For some reason, I would always forget to feed and water them. So my dad came up with a plan, which he shared with me at the supper table one evening. He said, "Every day you forget to feed the chickens we will give you a spanking adding one more swat each time. The first day, it will be one swat. The next time you forget, it will be two. Then three, four, etc. The chickens will have to be fed before supper." Unfortunately my forgetfulness continued. I came to the supper table one evening and it dawned on me, "Oh no! I forgot to feed the chickens! Again!" It would now be five swats. Immediately after supper I ran upstairs and devised a plan. I would pile on the underwear, putting on as many pairs as I could while looking inconspicuous. As I scrambled to pull up my pants over my four or five layers of underwear, my dad came up the steps, down the hall, turned into my bedroom, then asked me, "Did you feed the chickens today?" Feeling pretty confident the consequences would not be as bad as my dad thought they would be, I tried to put on a bit of a guilty face and replied, "No, I'm sorry. I forgot." My dad looked pretty disappointed and said, "We're up to five now, so go out to the shop and I'll be there shortly." The shop was a garage with additional space and a workbench. I knew it as the place where I endured most of my spankings. I went out to the shop still a bit nervous, not knowing if my plan would actually work. Then my dad came out with *the board* in hand and told me to bend over. When I did, he must have seen that my rump was a little more "rumpier" than normal. He gave me five swats…across the backs of my legs! Oh, that hurt.

Real correction hurts. I never got to six in a row, by the way. Sometimes we need reproof—a wrong brought to light. Other times, God brings a scourge to drive out our foolishness or train us to run well. No matter what kind of discipline God brings into our lives, we must always respect Him.

It is for discipline that you endure; God deals with you as with sons; for what son is there whom his father does not discipline? But if you are without discipline, of which all have become partakers, then you are illegitimate children and not sons. Furthermore, we had earthly fathers to discipline us, and we respected them; shall we not much rather be subject to the Father of spirits, and live? (Hebrews 12:7–9)

"Earthly fathers" is literally "fathers of the flesh," which contrasts with "Father of spirits." When we subject ourselves to the Lord, it means we are committed to Him. And when we commit ourselves to Him, look what happens:

> Furthermore, we had earthly fathers to discipline us, and we respected them; shall we not much rather be subject to the Father of spirits, and live? (Hebrews 12:9)

Those last two words are so important, "and live." We experience *living* as God desires for us. We experience what God wants for our lives. That is spelled out in the next five verses.

First, living means sharing in God's holiness.

> For they disciplined us for a short time as seemed best to them, but He disciplines us for our good, so that we may share His holiness. (Hebrews 12:10)

If we allow God to mold us and submit to Him, trusting Him even when times are tough, God will develop His holiness in us.

Second, to truly live means knowing God's amazing peace. Peace is the fruit that He will produce in us.

> All discipline for the moment seems not to be joyful, but sorrowful; yet to those who have been trained by it, afterwards it yields the peaceful fruit of righteousness. (Hebrews 12:11)

In my early twenties, newly married and in college, I had a mentor, our pastor named Don DenHartog. A few months after my wife and I got to know Don and his wife, the church went through a split. Sadly, Don received some very vicious verbal attacks and character assassination. I saw this pastor cling to the Lord in the midst of an incredibly difficult time. He is a man whom I have looked up to and respected for years, and I saw God use that trying season in his life to grow the peaceful fruit of righteousness in his life. We can have that same fruit produced in our lives as we stay committed to the course and the coach in the race that God has called us to run.

The third way God wants us to live is by experiencing real, deep, and lasting healing in our lives.

Therefore, strengthen the hands that are weak and the knees that are feeble, and make straight paths for your feet, so that the limb which is lame may not be put out of joint, but rather be healed. (Hebrews 12:12–13)

None of us is whole or complete. We are all broken and lame in some way. God wants to bring healing. If we trust Him to train us, according to these verses, He will use others to strengthen and mature us. When we see God making us whole and healing us deep within, that's living!

Fourth (I really love this one), experiencing the life God desires for us happens by seeing God.

Pursue peace with all men, and the sanctification without which no one will see the Lord. (Hebrews 12:14)

This is speaking about seeing God right now actively working. When we see God saving people, giving them victory in their lives, changing them, transforming their hearts, or showing us a life that is unexplainable apart from Him, then we are really living!

There's one more thing that God has established in order to help us run well: He has given us each other and we are called to run together.

See to it that no one comes short of the grace of God; that no root of bitterness springing up causes trouble, and by it many be defiled; (Hebrews 12:15)

This verse starts out by telling us to look out for one another because there is so much in life that can bring us down and cause us to become bitter. If there is one place where we need to be encouragers, it is in the church, among the body of believers. We need to help each other see the grace of God and how He acts for our good. It's hard to make sense of a lot of things in life, but one thing we can be clear on: God's motivation for how He operates is always out of grace. What motivates Him to do what He does comes from His infinite goodness to us, even though we don't deserve it. If we allow bitterness to creep into our relationships, it will harm our ability to live in the grace of God. That is why this verse warns us against animosity toward each other. If we let bitterness, resentment, or anger creep in, it is like the roots of crabgrass: it will grow out and spread until it takes over. We cannot let that happen.

If we are going to run this course well together, then we must challenge each other to stay on the path that God desires for us.

> that there be no immoral or godless person like Esau, who sold his own birthright for a single meal. For you know that even afterwards, when he desired to inherit the blessing, he was rejected, for he found no place for repentance, though he sought for it with tears. (Hebrews 12:16–17)

It may seem peculiar to us that right after the author warns against bitterness, because it will hinder our ability to experience the grace of God, he would mention Esau. The point being made to these Jewish Christians who were very familiar with the story of Esau is that he exchanged a genuine experience of the grace of God—truly living and knowing His blessings—for a fleeting fulfillment of his appetites. This resulted in him becoming bitter toward God and his brother, Jacob.

We are called as a church family to deal with people in our congregation who are acting immorally or in ways that have no regard for God (Matthew 18:15–20; 1 Corinthians 5:1–13). Esau did not have a repentant heart—a humble heart. He cared only about getting a blessing from his father (Genesis 27:36). Anyone who blatantly lives contrary to God's truth, any arrogance that goes against God, any sin that so easily entangles us, any encumbrance—God wants to strip it all away. And He calls us, as His children, to allow ourselves to be used by Him to address it. The reason why God wants to clean these things up and strip them away from our lives is because they get in the way of experiencing His grace. They cause us to fall short of His grace or fall short of seeing how He works for our good—how He moves in our lives to make us more holy, producing the peaceful fruit of righteousness and bringing about healing deep in our souls. We are called to make every effort to ensure that no one falls short of these things. So we address immorality because we want people to live in God's grace.

God's plan is that Christians live together as a church family, to look out for each other and encourage each other. The atmosphere He desires to create through us is a place where people can learn what it means to truly live in God's grace. God calls us to run this race with endurance and to run together. It is good to ask the questions "Who am I running with? Who do I allow to know me well enough to help me not fall short of God's grace? And who am I helping to run this race that God has set out for us?" If we run well together, things that encumber us will fall off and we will know the blessings of God's goodness in our lives.

CHAPTER TWENTY

ARE WE LISTENING?

Hebrews 12:18–29

I used to drive a deep-red 1996 Cadillac I picked up for a song at an auction our church held to raise money for a youth mission trip. I called it *My Sweet Ride*. It had electric leather seats, a digital dashboard that would tell you about everything happening with the car, a 32-valve, 8-cylinder, 300-horsepower Northstar engine. When I sat behind the wheel, the car would just float down the road. For all the sweet things *My Sweet Ride* had, one thing it did not come with was a great radio. It had the original stereo in it, but some of the radio stations I liked to listen to did not come in very well. While listening to one station, another would come in over the top of it. I would be listening to two stations at once, only hearing a bunch of noisy confusion. Other times, static would overpower the station and I would end up getting nothing but distortion.

The radio static in *My Sweet Ride* may be how many of us listen today: we have a lot of sounds we tune into all at the same time. We hear a person talking while we are texting or singing with the music pumping through our ear buds or reading a magazine or watching television. Good listening is like tuning into a radio station: for best results, listen to only one station at a time and get rid of all the static. But that is easier said than done.

Throughout the book of Hebrews the author calls his readers to connect with Christ in order to be His companions. In order for this to happen, we must be able to listen to Him and hear what He is saying to us. I wonder, how we are doing? Are we listening well, or do other noises overpower Him? Are we attempting to pay attention to more than one station at a time? How are we doing with our connection? Do we have good reception? Does God come in clearly?

As we move into the second half of Hebrews 12, the author starts by clarifying contrasts in connecting with God. God hasn't always communicated with His people in the same way. In the time of the New Testament until today, God's method has changed from His ways of the Old Testament.

As we read the first four verses (Hebrews 12:18–21), imagine you hear ominous or eerie music that typically plays in a suspenseful movie. Imagine the violins being played boldly, the kettledrums rumbling, the woodwinds clashing with their chords, as if something really big or maybe frightening is going to happen.

> For you have not come to a mountain that can be touched and to a blazing fire, and to darkness and gloom and whirlwind, and to the blast of a trumpet and the sound of words which sound was such that those who heard begged that no further word be spoken to them. For they could not bear the command, "If even a beast touches the mountain, it will be stoned." And so terrible was the sight, that Moses said, "I am full of fear and trembling." (Hebrews 12:18–21)[70]

With the music in our minds helping us feel the emotion of being quite terrified, we just read of darkness, gloom, and a whirlwind. Now let's change the music in our minds to something light and warm, like a ray of sun piercing through the clouds and beaming down on the Scriptures as we read the next three verses.

> But you have come to Mount Zion and to the city of the living God, the heavenly Jerusalem, and to myriads of angels, to the general assembly and church of the firstborn who are enrolled in heaven, and to God, the Judge of all, and to the spirits of the righteous made perfect, and to Jesus, the mediator of a new covenant, and to the sprinkled blood, which speaks better than the blood of Abel. (Hebrews 12:22–24)

In our translation, verse 22 into 23 says, "To myriads of angels, to

---

[70] See also Exodus 19:12–19.

the general assembly..." I think the English Standard Version captures this translation better: "To innumerable angels in festal gathering..." The Friberg Lexicon helps us understand this Greek word translated "festal gathering" in the ESV and "general assembly" in our translation (don't feel like you need to be able to read and understand the following Greek letters and words; just focus on the English and how this rare Greek word is translated): "πανήγυρις, εως, ἡ literally, as a festal gathering of a whole group *celebration, happy festive occasion*; καὶ μυριάσιν ἀγγέλων πανηγύρει *and to innumerable angels in joyful assembly* (HE 12.22)."[71] This gathering of so many angels was not just an assembling together, it was a celebration for what verse 23 describes: "And to the spirits of the righteous made perfect," or those who have gone before us in heaven as the author laid out in Hebrews 11.

To understand verse 24, we need to go back to Genesis 4:11. When Cain killed Abel, God said to Cain, "Now you are cursed from the ground, which has opened its mouth to receive your brother's blood from your hand." Abel's blood speaks of vengeance, justice, and the curse. The blood of Jesus speaks of forgiveness, pardon, and grace.

Here is the point of the contrasting feelings of these two sections of Hebrews 12:18–21 and then 12:22–24: What would you be more prone to listen to—God shaking the ground with a fear-instilling voice from heaven (as He did in the Old Testament), or the gentle, gracious nudging and prodding of God (as He has done since the inception of the church)?[72]

The stage is set for the fifth of five warnings in the book of Hebrews.[73] God operates and communicates out of His grace by

---

[71] Friberg, *Analytical Lexicon of the Greek New Testament*.

[72] Sometimes I feel as though we should go back to God shaking the ground and His terrifying voice being heard (and in the future we will, according to the Bible), but it's not like that now.

[73] There are five warnings to Christians throughout Hebrews:
   1. Don't drift! The danger of neglecting our salvation (2:1–4).
   2. Don't develop a hard heart and miss the kingdom rest (3:1–4:16).
   3. Beware of permanent dullness (5:11–6:20).
   4. Don't continue in willful sin (10:19–29).
   5. Don't fail to heed God's speaking (12:25–29).

nudging, prodding, and wooing. When He speaks, the warning is that we must listen.

See to it that you do not refuse Him who is speaking. (Hebrews 12:25a)

The phrase "who is speaking" is a present active participle, which means it is a continuous action in the present. God is not silent; He is still speaking today. We are called not to refuse, reject, or close our ears to Him.

A young man sat at his desk reflecting over the events that had taken place in the past couple of weeks. Being thrust into a position of national leadership had not come as a surprise, for leadership seemed to run in his family. His dad had been the nation's leader before him and had prepared him for the task as best he knew how. Now, the future well-being of the nation was on this young man's shoulders. Immediately he was confronted with several difficult decisions: primarily how to unite the nation now that his father had died and opportunists were creating dissent as the new leadership took over. Thankfully this young man's father had taught him to trust in the Lord because God would never fail him. He knew he had to turn to God, so he went on a retreat to a small private community nearby. In the evening as he lay on his bed, his body felt heavy as he began to relax, and he fell into a deep sleep. A vision entered his mind that was so vivid he knew it was more than a dream. In it, God spoke to him, saying, "Ask for whatever you want; I will give it to you." His mind raced with thoughts of what he would want as a new king: riches, power to control people, long life with perfect health? All along, an inner voice was persistent: "Wisdom to be an effective leader of our nation." So he prayed, "Lord, give your servant a listening heart so I can provide wise, effective leadership."

You may have picked up that this was a summary of the account of Solomon's rise to power as the king of Israel. The wisest man who ever lived knew, more than anything, that in order to be wise he must be a good listener. The last quote is from 1 Kings 3:9, where the words "a listening heart" are sometimes translated "an understanding heart." Literally, the word means to be a skilled listener. The same goes for us today. And the one to whom we ought to listen most is God Himself.

God speaks to us by way of three avenues. First is through the

Bible. This one seems obvious: The Bible is God's primary way to communicate to us. Think of the Bible as a letter God has written to us. God inspired the human authors (He moved them along by His Holy Spirit) to write His very words to us. Are we listening? Are we in His Word?

The second way God speaks to us is through prayer. James 1:5 says that if we lack wisdom, we are to ask God and He will give it to us generously. Philippians 4:6–7 says that if we are anxious, we are to pray and God's peace will come over us. And Romans 10:13 tells us to call on the Lord to be saved or rescued from sin. God clearly interacts with us and connects to us through prayer. Are we listening? Are we praying?

Finally, God speaks to us through others. God uses others to speak His truth into our lives. The Christian life was never meant to be lived alone. We need each other, to love one another in all purity. We must encourage, exhort, and push each other toward Jesus. Are we listening? Are we letting God use others to speak into our lives?

If you are like me, listening is hard. Do you realize that listening is not natural? We naturally hear, but to be a good listener takes work. And there are many obstacles that get in the way. Let me share five of them.[74]

First, we are poor listeners because we are defensive. God may want to speak to us through others, or through His Word, or through prayer, and we have a tendency to fight, deny, make excuses, or shift the blame. We are often quick to raise our defenses. Maybe we need to pull down our defenses and listen first without letting ourselves fight back in our minds. It may be a good discipline to just take it, absorb it, and understand that God may be speaking to us and wants us to learn from it.

The second obstacle is we would rather talk than listen. We are born with two ears and one mouth. That ought to tell us something. I find it fascinating that God has made us so we cannot close our ears but we can close our mouths. Here's an experiment to try some day: listen and see how much people love to talk (especially about themselves). We don't listen because we are too caught up in ourselves. We cannot

---

[74] Taken from Wakefield, *Perceptive Listening.*

listen to the Lord because we would rather listen to ourselves. Sometimes, I'm afraid, our mouths are obstacles to good listening.

Third, we are distracted. Like the radio in *My Sweet Ride*, so many competing voices, so much static, so many noises drown out the Lord. We have thousands of things on our minds: things to do, people to think about, situations to resolve in our heads, etc. These are internal distractions. We also have external distractions: TV, computers, smart phones, even the radio. How can we stop all the chaos and listen? God is speaking; are we listening?

Another hindrance to good listening is being tired. A 2008 study released by the Center for Disease Control (CDC) indicates that adults are not getting enough rest each night. Of those questioned, 70 percent said they had not gotten enough rest or sleep every day over the past month.[75] The National Sleep Foundation says we need seven to nine hours of sleep per night. Many adults average six or less. Late-night TV, Internet use, caffeine are just some of the things that get in the way of getting a good night's sleep. I know for me, when I am tired, my connection with the Lord is weakened because my tired mind cannot listen well.

The fifth obstacle to listening is we erect barriers. It is true that God speaks to us through others. However, we have a tendency to decide who we're going to allow God to speak through and who we are not. We may like a person so we feel God can use him or her to speak to us. But we may not like another person and so we choose to shut our ears. Yes, we must be discerning, making sure those we listen to align with the Bible, but to listen well, we need to understand God may even use our critics or people who rub us the wrong way to speak to us. Let's not put up barriers too quickly, because God may be trying to say something to us, and we need to ask, "Are we listening?"

There is a very good reason why we must listen to God: because God is watching.

See to it that you do not refuse Him who is speaking. For if those did not escape when they refused him who warned them on earth, much

---

[75] Wachter and Stark, "Tired?"

You can read about how those in the Old Testament who did not escape God's judgment when they refused to listen to Him (in Numbers 16; 21; and 25, to name a few). God was watching, and because the Israelites turned away from the Lord, He carried out His justice and discipline upon them. Notice in Hebrews 12:25 the author used the word "we." He included himself. As Christians, *we* can turn away from the Lord. *We* can stop listening to Him. The warning is this: God is still speaking and watching and He will carry out His justice, He will discipline us (remember the first half of Hebrews 12), even severely if needed. He is watching, so keep listening.

Another reason why we listen to the Lord is this world is temporary and He desires for us to think about the eternal. This world we live in continues to grab our attention, but all this world offers is like static on the radio. The busyness of our lives, being involved in so many things, and the things that we own (or that own us) are not bad in themselves, but where is God on the hierarchy of our lives? Is He at the top or somewhere down toward the bottom where we fit Him in whenever it is convenient? Things that try to drown out the Lord and pull us away from Him are all going to be gone one day.

And His voice shook the earth then, but now He has promised, saying, "Yet once more I will shake not only the earth, but also the heaven." (Hebrews 12:26)

In 1980, when I was fourteen, my family packed up the big station wagon and took a vacation out west. We stayed at KOA campsites along the way and hit all the "big dogs" that a family might make sure they visit—Mount Rushmore, Wall Drug, the Corn Palace in South Dakota, Custer's Last Stand in Little Bighorn, Montana—on our way out to see Mount Saint Helens, which had blown its top that year. My favorite stop had to be Yellowstone National Park. The bison, the bears, the elk, the mountains, all the heated sulfur-smelling pools, and, of course, the geysers like Old Faithful. For all of its beauty, Yellowstone may not be as nice as we think: The park sits atop a massive caldron of magma, its total volume enough to fill Lake Michigan more than three times. Yellowstone is known as a supervolcano. From 2004 to 2010 the ground levels over the volcano have risen ten inches in some places. Bob Smith, from the University of Utah and an expert on Yellowstone's volcanic activity, said, "It's an extraordinary uplift, because it covers such a large area and the rates are so high."[76] Maybe this supervolcano is just belching a little bit; we don't really know. What we do know is this earth is not as stable as we think. It wouldn't take much for God to release a supervolcano like Yellowstone and the prophecies of one-hundred-pound hailstones falling from the sky (Revelation 16:21) and this earth becoming consumed by fire (2 Peter 3:10) become a reality. So if we are going to invest our lives, doesn't it make sense to invest them in what is eternal rather than what is temporal or temporary?

> This expression, "Yet once more," denotes the removing of those things which can be shaken, as of created things, so that those things which cannot be shaken may remain. Therefore, since we receive a kingdom which cannot be shaken, let us show gratitude, by which we may offer to God an acceptable service with reverence and awe; for our God is a consuming fire. (Hebrews 12:27–29)

Our incredible God will consume everything that is not holy or that goes contrary to His perfect character. And one day His eternal kingdom will come! So let's live focused on Him and live for His kingdom. We have been made to connect with our eternal Almighty God; the only way we can connect with Him is if we listen to Him. We have to get rid of the static, work through the obstacles, tune out the competing noises, and work at what does not come naturally: truly listening to our Lord.

---

[76] Handwerk, "Yellowstone."

CHAPTER TWENTY-ONE

ACCEPTABLE SERVICE

Hebrews 13:1–14

Have you ever been at a family picnic, or a festival of some kind and tried to compete in a three-legged race? You pair up with another person, get out some soft rope or rags, and tie one of your legs to your partner's leg. Fumbling as you coordinate your steps with each other, you make your way to the starting line. The starter, seeing everyone is at the line, raises a hand, and says, "On your mark. Get set. *Go!*" Your partner and you jerk to get in step; it takes some doing. You yank each other a bit, wonder why you didn't practice before you started, and struggle to get in sync. After a few yards, however, you start to figure it out and find that you are striding together.

As we have been going through Hebrews, the message has been clear: "Be a companion with Christ." Which means we are to run with Him, be His partner, partake of this race with Him, and keep in step with Him. It is as if we are called to run a three-legged race with Jesus. As we move into the first half of the last chapter of the book, the author will give us five practical ways we can live out this companionship and stay in stride with our Lord.

The first way we can run this race with the Lord Jesus is by loving one another. Hebrews 13 starts this way:

Let love of the brethren continue. (Hebrews 13:1)

This can be a challenge. Like the beginning of the three-legged race, we can have a hard time getting in step with each other in our relationships. We all have our quirks, and if we are around each other long enough, we can begin to get annoyed. If we do not keep our emotions in check, it can lead to becoming irritated. If our irritation goes unrestrained, we will end up having a lack of love for each other. If love came easy, this verse would not have been written.

How do we love one another on a practical level? The next two verses will help clarify this. First, Hebrews 13:2:

> Do not neglect to show hospitality to strangers, for by this some have entertained angels without knowing it. (Hebrews 13:2)

The church back then was experiencing persecution, driving Christians far and wide. There were no hotels like we have today, so it was common for people to need places to stay while traveling.

The word used for "hospitality" here is really two Greek words put together. The root of the word means to show hospitality; however, added to the root is the word *phileo*, which means "brotherly love." "Hospitality" here did not just mean putting someone up for the night (which the root word alone would indicate as it is used in Acts 28:23 and Philemon 1:22). It meant to show others love by letting them know you care. We are to show hospitality in order to communicate brotherly love toward others.

This whole notion of entertaining angels without even knowing presents a challenge to know precisely what the author was meaning. The original Greek word is the plural form of *angelos*. It can be translated "angels." However, it can also be translated "messengers." As Christians moved from city to city, some of them carried letters from one church to another with messages. Therefore, the end of Hebrews 13:2 could have very easily been understood by the first recipients of this letter that as they showed hospitality, they may have the opportunity to entertain messengers from other churches. I'm comfortable with that interpretation of this verse. That being said, the way that most English translations have chosen to use the word "angels" is legitimate as well.

To love one another also meant to come alongside of other Christians when they were being mistreated.

Remember the prisoners, as though in prison with them, and those who are ill-treated, since you yourselves also are in the body. (Hebrews 13:3)

In the early 1990s a pro-life leader was put in a prison close to where I grew up in Franklin, Wisconsin, in a facility called the House of Correction (HOC).[77] My dad said, "Come with me. We are going to visit him." I didn't even know the man and my dad didn't either. But my dad said, "The Bible tells us to visit the prisoners." It was the first time I had stepped into the inner walls of a prison. The man, Joseph Foreman, was brought out to us. My dad made some small talk with him and was sure to tell him we were praying for him. The man had not done anything violent or harmed anyone in any way when he protested abortion. He was humble and kind and grateful for our visit. That was also the first time I witnessed a Christian who was mistreated just for being bold about his faith.

If we know Christians who are in prison or mistreated either here or around the world, it is good to ask ourselves, "How can I communicate that I love them and care for them?" If we are going to be companions with Christ, we must love one another.

The second way to be a companion with Christ has to do with marriage: we must keep marriage sacred. We do not have to look far to see that our society wages war against the sacredness of sexual intercourse and God's design that it is to be practiced only in the context of marriage. The vast majority of Americans have had sex outside of marriage and feel it is perfectly fine to live together as unmarried couples. As a result, births to unmarried women have skyrocketed in the last few decades. Our world does not agree with the next verse in Hebrews.

Marriage is to be held in honor among all, and the marriage bed is to be undefiled; for fornicators and adulterers God will judge. (Hebrews 13:4)

I don't think God's Word can be clearer. What we see in our society is wrong. We have moved far away from what this verse says. I am convinced many Christians have moved away from treating marriage

---

[77] That was its name back then. Today it is called the County Correctional Facility South (CCF-S).

and the marriage bed with this kind of reverence. The 1960s brought about a counterculture of "free love" and anything goes, lowering the standards of respect for the institution of marriage and the sacred activities that are reserved for married couples. It is time to have another countercultural movement where we stand up for purity. Marriage and the marriage bed are sacred. Marriage is the creation of God for our well-being as individuals and for our society. If marriage and the marriage bed break down, people become immoral, which leads to being untrustworthy. Relationships are weakened and all of society slips into decay physically, emotionally, and spiritually. To dishonor God's design for marriage is to dishonor God. And in the end "fornicators and adulterers God will judge."

The third way to keep in step with Jesus—to be his companion—is to trust Him explicitly.

> Make sure that your character is free from the love of money, being content with what you have; for He Himself has said, "I will never desert you, nor will I ever forsake you," so that we confidently say, "The Lord is my helper, I will not be afraid. What will man do to me?" (Hebrews 13:5–6)

Erwin Rommel was the most famous German general of both World War I and World War II. He was called the "Desert Fox" for his sly genius in North Africa. He was loyal to his leaders throughout both world wars, including Adolf Hitler. Hitler said Rommel was his favorite general. Rommel was loyal to his soldiers, refusing to force them into battles he knew they would lose. He was a hero in Germany. Even when he disagreed with Hitler, he opposed any assassination plots he may have heard about. In July 1944, the Gestapo uncovered a plot to kill Hitler, and under torture one of the conspirators turned on Rommel and said he was a part of it. Hitler asked Rommel about his participation. Rommel truthfully denied involvement, but Hitler betrayed his most trustworthy general by giving him a choice: take poison and his family would be spared, or go to trial and his family would face the firing squad. Rommel chose the poison.

General Erwin Rommel is not alone in history. People betray people all the time. The idea that our Lord will never betray us may be hard for us to truly trust because, if you are like me, you have had experiences where people we have trusted and given your heart to have turned their backs on you. Only Jesus can say, "I will never desert you, nor will I ever forsake you."

Who or what are we putting our trust in? The author of Hebrews says not to trust in money for our well-being but to be content with what the Lord gives us. We have a tendency to put our trust in people for our well-being. If our parents, siblings, or friends show us that we are accepted, we feel good and have a healthy self-image. If we are rejected, we feel like we don't make the grade as a person. These verses tell us that every person, our worldly possessions, virtually everything except Jesus can and probably will forsake us. To be a companion with Christ means we place our trust in Him and make Him the foundation of our lives.

Upon the foundation of trust in Jesus, the fourth way to partake in Him is to always watch and learn.

> Remember those who led you, who spoke the word of God to you; and considering the result of their conduct, imitate their faith. (Hebrews 13:7)

The Bible says the Word of God must be preached and that transformation happens in people as they hear the Word proclaimed (Romans 10:14–15; 2 Timothy 4:1–2). Yet the conduct of the preacher or teacher is more important than what they teach. No matter if it is a famous preacher, a Sunday school teacher, or a mentor, the reality is that conduct matters. The apostle Paul said two things: "Be imitators of me, just as I also am of Christ" (1 Corinthians 11:1) and "It is a trustworthy statement, deserving full acceptance, that Christ Jesus came into the world to save sinners, among whom I am foremost of all" (1 Timothy 1:15). Putting those two together, Paul was saying, "If you see Christ in me, imitate what you see; but know that I am a sinner too." It is about being an open book, being real, not hiding our weaknesses, failures, and struggles. At the same time, we must be honest and open about how Jesus is working in our lives and the victories we experience as we live in His grace.

One of the struggles with preachers and teachers on the radio, television, or on the Internet is we do not know how they are living their lives. They may be great teachers, but what are their lives like, their marriages, families, the way they treat others? The author of Hebrews is saying, "Don't just learn from the material that is taught, learn from what you see in the lives of spiritual leaders. Learn from how they live lives of trusting in the Lord and partnering with Him." Watch leaders, teachers, and preachers; how they live matters more than what they teach. And "imitate their faith."

A fifth way to be a companion of Christ is to be strengthened by His grace.

> Jesus Christ is the same yesterday and today and forever. Do not be carried away by varied and strange teachings; for it is good for the heart to be strengthened by grace… (Hebrews 13:8–9a)

If we are weak physically, we know what to do: we lift weights, do push-ups and some sit-ups, and maybe pick up running or biking. What if we are weak in grace; do we know what to do? How can we "be strengthened by grace"? If we want to be strong and stay strong, we have to keep doing our push-ups, sit-ups, and aerobic exercises. The same is true with grace; we have to continue working out in grace.

Three different grace exercises are critical to staying strong. First, we must remain in the truth about grace. If you grew up in a home where you felt you could never measure up or were often put down, it will be hard for you to receive God's grace. If you feel you have to earn God's love or feel you don't deserve it, you will never grasp God's grace. If you believe that God loves you, yet He holds some of His love back from you because you don't measure up to His expectations, then God's grace will feel out of reach for you. Those kinds of feelings and thoughts are built on lies. To be strong in grace, we must combat those misconceptions with the truth.

> Do not be carried away by varied and strange teachings; for it is good for the heart to be strengthened by grace, not by foods, through which those who were so occupied were not benefited. (Hebrews 13:9)

It is hard to believe that our Lord accepts us and we don't have to do anything to deserve it—nothing! It is hard to trust that after God the Father has brought us into His eternal family we do not have to do anything to prove that we are saved. Because of God's grace, He shows us favor, love, forgiveness, and mercy without us earning it in any way. This is the truth about God's grace, and we must be forever strengthened in it.

A second exercise to stay strong in grace is to keep focused on Jesus. It is extremely tempting for many to add to the gospel (the good news about Jesus) or to look to our behavior for reasons why we are acceptable to the Lord. To stay strong in grace, we must reject anything that is added to the gospel and always bring ourselves back to Jesus and what He has done for us.

> We have an altar from which those who serve the tabernacle have no right to eat. For the bodies of those animals whose blood is brought into the holy place by the high priest as an offering for sin, are burned outside the camp. Therefore Jesus also, that He might sanctify the people through His own blood, suffered outside the gate. (Hebrews 13:10–12)

To stay focused on Jesus is to proclaim in our hearts and to the world around us that Jesus died for us. Jesus died so that the penalty for your sin and my sin was paid for. God the Father forgives you and me because God the Son, Jesus, died in our place. We can know God personally and grow in our relationship with Him all because of what Jesus has done for each of us.

One last discipline to stay strong in grace: we must exercise humility.

> So, let us go out to Him outside the camp, bearing His reproach. (Hebrews 13:13)

Do you know who were put outside the camp? The rejected. Typically it was the Sabbath breakers, the blasphemers (Leviticus 24), and the lepers (Numbers 5:2). To be outside the camp meant you were humbled. The types of people who were rejected were forced to go outside the camp. Notice, however, in Hebrews 13:13, going outside the camp was a voluntary activity.

The author of Hebrews is calling his readers to come out to the Lord humbly, knowing that we are not worthy of acceptance. We are to come to the Lord abandoning our self-righteousness and pious arrogance or holier-than-thou attitudes. When we come before Jesus, we must come as broken vessels fully owning our need for His grace. When we live this way, we will be strengthened in His grace.

When we are practicing these five ways to serve the Lord (love one another, keep marriage sacred, trust Jesus explicitly, always watch and learn, and be strengthened by the grace of Christ), we will know that we have companionship with Jesus. We will be in step with Him, partnering with and partaking in Him.

This three-legged race being tied to Jesus is all about running to finish the race when we get to heaven.

> For here we do not have a lasting city, but we are seeking the city which is to come. (Hebrews 13:14)

How are we doing in this race? Are we tied tightly to Jesus? Are we His companions? Let us run and not stop. If we are not in sync, we will fall. If we do not keep in step, we will falter. So let us run—all the way until the end—as companions, partakers, and partners with Christ.

CHAPTER TWENTY-TWO

A COMMUNITY COMMITTED TO BEING CHRIST'S COMPANIONS

Hebrews 13:15–25

My first full-time job after I graduated from high school was a construction job. The man I worked for did remodeling, drywall, and all types of carpentry work. I loved that work and learned a great deal from the owner of the company. What made construction so satisfying was the feeling of accomplishment because there were such tangible outcomes. It would start with a plan, a drawing, or a picture. These drawings would lay out a hope of what the construction job would end up looking like: a new addition, a changed floor plan, or a remodeled room. In the end, when the job was done, we could clearly see the results of our work.

As we come to the end of this incredible book of Hebrews, we will see that Jesus has drawn up a plan or a blueprint—a hope for all the churches. Throughout the whole book what it means to be companions with Christ has been the theme. To end the book the author lays out the hope for all churches to commit to being partners with Jesus. The challenge is to take this plan—this blueprint—and make it a reality. How do we construct our churches so that we are in tune with Jesus and committed to being His companions? How do we take what looks good on paper, written down in the Bible, and make it tangible?

191

To construct a community that partners with Christ, we must integrate into our churches a commitment to building the right tone. Tone is so critical. It's the feeling people get when they are around us. If asked, many would suggest that to have a great church we need a great vision, or we need to make sure that the Bible is central to all we do. I couldn't argue against either of those; both are so important. However, what is even more foundational (or primal) for the health of the church is to have an atmosphere with a positive feeling or tone. This tone is driven by the incredible calling we have to partner with Jesus and to make a difference in our day for His glory. Jesus has called us to play a significant role in His eternal plans.

So strap on the tool belt, throw in the tools, look at the blueprints of the end of Hebrews, and let's begin this construction project by working on our tone as each individual local church. To nail down the right tone, we start by praising God.

> Through Him then, let us continually offer up a sacrifice of praise to God, that is, the fruit of lips that give thanks to His name. (Hebrews 13:15)

As children of God, we are called to share out loud with others what Jesus has done. With our "lips," let us not be ashamed to praise God "continually."

Often, when we as Christians share about our lives, we will either talk about a struggle we are having, or we will say we are doing fine. It is rare that we share things to praise God for. Big things we talk about: getting engaged, or having a baby, but we normally don't share smaller things because it feels like we are bragging. "Praise God I got a raise!" "Praise God my kids are really enjoying the sport they are in!" "Praise God my marriage is pretty solid." James 1:17 says everything good and perfect is a gift from God above. He takes care of us financially, He gives us our health, He works in our relationships, He sanctifies us to be kinder, more gracious, and aligned with His truth. To construct a community that partners with Christ, we must look for opportunities to praise God; not bragging, yet setting the right tone of rejoicing with those who rejoice (Romans 12:15).

Another foundational pillar we must set in place is to love one another.

> And do not neglect doing good and sharing, for with such sacrifices God is pleased. (Hebrews 13:16)

Notice the word "sacrifices." To sacrifice means we get out of our comfort zones to do what pleases God. Sacrificing means we stretch ourselves. It means we go out of our way to be generous, caring, and loving. My wife and I went out one night for a brief date to get a piece of pie and a coffee at a local restaurant. As we were being led to our seats, we happened upon another couple from our church who seemed to have had the same idea. We visited momentarily, and then Jill and I went to our table to enjoy our time together. When we went to pay our bill, the waitress said another couple had picked up our tab. That was so loving of them. It is an example of a way to sacrifice to do good and share. As a community of believers, each local church must work at creating a tone where others sense that we really love each other.

Here is a proper tone setter that can be a challenge for some but is imperative if we want to be a community that is committed to being Christ's companions: follow the leaders. The next verse starts out:

> Obey your leaders and submit to them... (Hebrews 13:17a)

The idea of submitting to leaders is not very popular today because there have been some bad leaders in some churches. Yet look at the responsibility the leaders have:

> Obey your leaders and submit to them, for they keep watch over your souls as those who will give an account. Let them do this with joy and not with grief, for this would be unprofitable for you. (Hebrews 13:17)

God doesn't want us to follow bad leaders who head in the wrong direction. When looking at leaders, ask, "Are they in it for themselves? Do they love power? Are they money focused?" If you answer in the affirmative on these types of questions, don't follow them. Also ask, "Are they gentle, levelheaded, peaceable, and holding to God's faithful Word and sound doctrine? Do they love God and love others?" Even though you may not agree with them, if these kinds of things define them, obey and follow them. For they have to give an account one day before the Lord, and this verse says we must help them lead with joy.

We will be making sure the tone in the church will be right as we—together—construct a community of Christ's companions.

If we want to build a community of Christ's companions, we must also be committed to prayer. The church is pictured as a family. Words like "brethren," "household," or "children of God" are used often when the Bible speaks of the church. And families who pray together, stay together.

As a church family, people of each local church must pray for their leaders. Look at the prayer request in the next verse:

> Pray for us, for we are sure that we have a good conscience, desiring to conduct ourselves honorably in all things. (Hebrews 13:18)

The author was requesting prayer for the leaders (including himself—"Pray for *us*"). Not because there was a big hurdle they had to get over or a problem they had to address. The request was laid before the church community because the leaders wanted to grow in being honorable. Therefore, leaders in the church need our prayers. This is a spiritual battle we are in, and leaders need the children of God to pray for them. Prayer makes a difference, and the author knew it.

> And I urge you all the more to do this, so that I may be restored to you the sooner. (Hebrews 13:19)

Pray for the leaders (Hebrews 13:18), and the author asked specifically to pray for him (here in verse 19). He had a heart for them as he longed to be with them. He knew if the recipients of his letter would pray for his situation, God would work through their prayers.

To build a community committed to being Christ's companions, not only are the people of the church to pray for the leaders, but also the leaders are to pray for the people of the church.

> Now the God of peace, who brought up from the dead the great Shepherd of the sheep through the blood of the eternal covenant, even Jesus our Lord, equip you in every good thing to do His will, working in us that which is pleasing in His sight, through Jesus Christ, to whom be the glory forever and ever. Amen. (Hebrews 13:20–21)

Notice at the beginning of verse 21 our translation reads, "Equip you." That same original Greek word is used in Matthew 4:21 and Mark 1:19 for *mending* nets in order to make them useful. The same word is used in Galatians 6:1 for those who are spiritual to *restore* those caught up in sin. And in 1 Thessalonians 3:10, Paul, and those with him, wanted to *complete* what was lacking in the faith of those he was writing to. From all these different ways of using this Greek verb we can get the sense of taking what is not complete, or broken in some way, and mending it. It is developing other people so that they are completely adapted for God's intended use for them. Oh, that church leaders would passionately pray for this for the people God has placed under their care. Churches can have programs, they can have great social gatherings, and mentoring can be happening, but if we are not praying, all the things we are doing will lack the spiritual vitality God desires for them. To construct a community committed to being Christ's companions, we must be committed to prayer.

Finally, to finish this construction project, we must be committed to growing.

I played the French horn from third grade through tenth grade. When I was in middle school, I joined the Milwaukee Pops Youth Band, which was a collection of musicians who really wanted to play well. I loved making that brass instrument sing, so much so that my parents paid for private lessons from a man who played in the Milwaukee Symphony Orchestra.

He used to push me every week, "How much are you practicing? You must practice at least an hour a day if you want to get better. It is imperative that you practice." I once asked him if he practiced every day still.

"Every day for a few hours."

"Why?"

"There is always room for improvement."

That is so true in many aspects of life. There is always room for improvement. In the most important relationship of our lives we must continue to improve in knowing and loving Jesus. As Christians, we must be committed to growing as His companions and practice every day to get better at it.

Toward the end of my French horn–playing days I stopped practicing consistently and rested on the abilities I had already acquired. Instead of staying at the level I was at, I actually drifted backward. The same will be true with our Christianity if we don't keep practicing. If we are not growing, we are dying; if we are not pushing forward, we are drifting backward. We must be committed to growing.

Therefore, we must allow the Word of God to penetrate and pierce our minds and hearts.

> But I urge you, brethren, bear with this word of exhortation, for I have written to you briefly. (Hebrews 13:22)

The words "urge" and "exhortation" are very similar sounding in the original language. I think the author was using a play on words, as if to say, "I *urge* you to listen carefully and let this strong *urging* penetrate your heart." The strong urging (exhortation) he was referring to was the whole book (yet the author added, "For I have written to you briefly"). The book of Hebrews (along with the other sixty-five books of the Bible) is God's Word. If we want to be a community committed to being Christ's companions, we must be men and women who crave the Word, who let it penetrate us and who allow it to sink not only into our minds but into our hearts as well. We must let God's Word transform us.

To continue to grow, we must allow accountability to motivate us. Accountability works only when people ask for it for themselves. The recipients of this book had some strong motivation to grow.

> Take notice that our brother Timothy has been released, with whom, if he comes soon, I will see you. Greet all of your leaders and all the saints. Those from Italy greet you. (Hebrews 13:23–24)

Sometimes when my wife, Jill, is away, I'll tell her that I will get the dishes done, or clean up around the house in her absence. Then she leaves and what do I do? I might plop down on the couch and veg out to television, or read a book, or do anything other than clean the house. That is until I know we are getting close to the time she will be coming home. Therein lies the motivation to get up and do what I promised.

The fact that the author and Timothy would, in a sense, be home soon meant the community there needed to take the message of

Hebrews seriously. It was as if the author said, "Listen, I'm on my way." Therefore, the recipients of the letter had this heightened urgency to live out the exhortations—the *urgings*—that the author had written *briefly* here.

To construct a community committed to being companions with Christ, we need to invite accountability into our lives. Therefore, churches must work at being communities in which openness and honesty are encouraged, people don't have to worry about being shamed, and serious motivation to progress as Christ's companions is a positive part of the culture.

Finally, to construct a community committed to growing as Christ's companions, in addition to letting the Word of God penetrate and accountability to motivate, we must allow grace to permeate. Grace must saturate each of us and all that we are as a church. I love the last line of the entire book:

Grace be with you all. (Hebrews 13:25)

Do you remember the nursery rhyme "Humpty Dumpty"? After Humpty fell, he had an unsolvable problem: all the king's horses and all the king's men couldn't put him back together again. We have a problem too, but our problem is solvable. I dug up a takeoff of this well-known nursery rhyme I remembered reading years ago:

Jesus Christ came to our wall,

Jesus Christ died for our fall;

So that regardless of death and in spite of our sin,

Through grace, He might put us together again.

There is so much joy being in God's grace, being His delight, and being His pleasure. It is God's grace that molds us, mends us, and puts us back together again. The only way we can be Christ's companions is by His grace. Because He has shown us grace, may grace be with us all.

As I said at the beginning of this chapter, in my late teens I did construction work. I can still remember a job my boss sent me to do that had no plans, no drawings, no instructions, and no leadership. I was told to go and add on an extension to a shed. I didn't know what I was doing, and my boss didn't give me any guidance. Needless to say, the results were pretty bad. The roofline was crooked, the walls didn't match up, and the whole construction was not very solid.

To construct this companionship with Christ, we have the plans written down and we have leaders on the jobsite to guide us. We just have to commit to doing the job. We have to work hard. We have to strap on our tool belts and contribute our efforts to build a community committed to being Christ's companions. If we start today, I guarantee (by the authority of the Bible) it will last forever.

CHAPTER DISCUSSION QUESTIONS

CHAPTER ONE

WHO IS THIS JESUS?

Hebrews 1:1–14

1. If you were to describe in a sentence what the Christian life is all about, what would you say? Is it different than what you would have said prior to reading chapter 1?

2. If you have a concordance, do a search on the words "Son of David" and see what that title means for Jesus. Also, look up 2 Samuel 7:8–17 (known as the Davidic Covenant). Some things in the passage seem to be talking about Solomon, but other things seem to be talking about Jesus. See if you can discern which is which.

3. Hebrews 1:6–8 makes it clear that Jesus will be King over the whole earth. How do you think that will be different from Jesus being King right now (or is He King right now)?

   Hebrews 1:6 says that Jesus is the "firstborn." Read Romans 8:29; Colossians 1:15, 18; and describe what it means that He is the "firstborn."

4. Hebrews 1:9 indicates that Jesus has companions. What it means to be His companions is a major theme throughout the book of Hebrews. Are you His companion? Explain.

5. Jesus is described as Creator, God, and sustainer (Hebrews 1:2–3, 8, 10–12). How do these descriptions impact you as a follower of Jesus?

   What did you think about the fact that the earth, as we know it, will perish (Hebrews 1:11–12)? Read 2 Peter 3:10–13. What does that passage say will be the environment of the new heavens and new earth? Compare and contrast how our earth is now and how it will be in eternity.

6. Hebrews 1:3 says Jesus made purification of our sins. Share with the group things in your life that Jesus has purified you from. Share the impact that His paying the penalty for your sin has had on your life.

Chapter Two

AVOIDING THE BLAHS

Hebrews 2:1–8

1. We are all prone to get the "blahs" at certain times in our lives. On a scale of 1 to 10 (1 being zero- blah, 10 being super-blah), how are you feeling these days: Do you have the "blahs"? What triggers them?

2. According to Hebrews 2:1, we're not supposed to get the blahs in our walk with the Lord. How does the *drifting away* happen in your life?

3. If we neglect our salvation (Hebrews 2:2–3a), God will correct us. The word "penalty" (in the original language of Greek) shows up only two other times in the Bible: Hebrews 10:35 and 11:26. Read those other passages within their context and see if you can determine what kind of penalty the author of Hebrews was referring to (i.e., when this penalty will take place, and to whom will this penalty be given). How does that motivate you?

    Now read Hebrews 12:3–11. According to this text, the Lord may correct us even now. Have you ever known the Lord's correction (or discipline) in your life? Explain. How can we tell the difference between the Lord's discipline and just a trial that we are going through (James 1:2–4)?

4. Hebrews 2:3–8 tells us why we must never take our salvation lightly. We are connected to the past (our forefathers in the faith), we have a responsibility for the present (to carry the light of the Lord), and we have a future—our destiny (dominion over God's creation). In light of these truths, how might you want to live differently from this day forward?

   Do you know what your spiritual gifts are (Hebrews 2:4)? Are you using your spiritual gifts to build up and edify the body of Christ—the church (Romans 12:3–13; 1 Corinthians 12:1–31; Ephesians 4:11–16)?

5. How much do you think about your eternal destiny: what you will be doing in all of eternity? Later chapters in Hebrews will give us a clearer picture of what our eternal destiny looks like. For now, when you hear "How you live today matters for eternity," does it inspire you at all? Why or why not?

CHAPTER THREE

THE PERFECT

Hebrews 2:9–18

1. Are you a perfectionist? Do you know a perfectionist? Is being a perfectionist a good thing or a bad thing? Explain.

2. Scripture tells us that Jesus is the only and perfect way to be in glory one day (Hebrews 2:9–10). What about the people in the remote parts of Africa or Asia or South America (anywhere in the world) who have never heard about Jesus—do you think they will be in heaven? Does Romans 1:18–23 pertain to them?

3. The motivation behind our salvation is God's grace (Hebrews 2:9). Why is grace so amazing to you? Or if it's not, why?

4. Hebrews 2:11 says that Jesus is the One who sanctifies us. What does "sanctify" mean? How do you call on Jesus to sanctify you? Have you seen His victory in your life lately? Why or why not do you think?

5. Jesus is our perfect helper (Hebrews 2:14–18). One of the ways He helps us is by setting us free from fear (Hebrews 2:15–16).

   a. Have you ever compromised your moral choices because of fear? Why is fear such a strong motivator?

b. Read John 8:36. Have you had this kind of a life with Jesus? If not, how can Christians come alongside each other to know the freedom we are to have in Christ? How does grace come in and play a role in our relationships with each other?

Chapter Four

OUR HEAVENLY CALLING

Hebrews 3:1–19

1. Read Hebrews 3:1. How does knowing you have been given a "heavenly calling" stir your heart and mind?

2. The word "consider" (NIV says "fix your thoughts") in Hebrews 3:1 means to be a deep thinker about Jesus. Have you been a student of Jesus? How have you been engaged in learning about Him lately? Or, if you have not been a student lately, what might you do to become one? What might be your next step?

3. It appears that, according to Hebrews 3:6, it is our heavenly calling to be the church. Is it possible to be Christians who gather together and not be the church? Why or why not?

   a. Hebrews 3:6 tells us to "hold fast" (NIV 1984 says "hold on to") our confidence (see also Hebrews 3:14). Here are some other passages that use the same Greek word to help us understand what "hold fast" means: Luke 8:15; 1 Corinthians 11:2; 15:2; 1 Thessalonians 5:21; Hebrews 10:23. How do those passages help you understand what it means to "hold fast"? How are you doing at this?

   b. Do you remember what we must be doing if we are to be

the church (Hebrews 3:7–13)? Remember the description of encouragers as superheroes? Are you a part of a church where supermen and wonder women encourage in accordance with Hebrews 3:12–13? How can we be better at this?

4. According to Hebrews 3:14, how can we be a "partaker of Christ"?

What words do other translations use for what the New American Standard Bible translates "assurance" in this verse? Do other translations help us understand what that means? Are you clinging to or holding fast to assurance?

5. Why didn't the Israelites enter into the Promised Land (described as God's rest in Hebrews 3:11, 18) according to Hebrews 3:15–19 (especially verse 19)? This is not speaking about the free gift of salvation; yet it seems to be tied to what the Israelites did—their actions. How consistent are you in your faith? How consistent are you in living out your heavenly calling? How can Christians be the church and help each other in becoming more consistent?

CHAPTER FIVE

GOD'S REST

Hebrews 4:1–16

1. How *crazy* is your life? Are you like those gerbils that you read about at the beginning of the chapter? Do you agree or disagree with this statement: "Doing has become our identity"? Why?

2. In Hebrews 4:1–5, the author of Hebrews seems to say that to know God's rest in our lives is a choice. Remember the illustration about lifting weights in high school? Those Jewish Christians needed the weight of the law lifted off them—the "dos" and "don'ts." When you think about your Christian walk, do you think you are a legalist, or do you know anyone who is? How can we avoid getting sucked into the trap of legalism?

3. Hebrews 4:6 warns us not to be "disobedient." Remember the description of that word? If you were to swing the pendulum of your life, would you swing more toward legalism or more toward being headstrong (or obstinate) when it comes to listening to God (Hebrews 4:7)?

4. Read Hebrews 4:8–9 where the word "Sabbath" is added to "rest." The chapter said that Sabbath is a counterbalance to the elements of our lives. The point was we need to stop doing what

we normally do and realign ourselves with God. How often do you do that?

5. Read Hebrews 4:10–11. How diligent are you in your relationship with God?

    a. Read Hebrews 4:12–13. How would you assess your diligence in your hearing/reading of God's Word, for the purposes that He lays out in these verses?

    b. Read Hebrews 4:13 and note the last phrase. Now read those last six or so words from different translations. Do you remember how the chapter described it? How has your relationship with the Lord been lately?

6. These last three verses sum up what God's rest is (Hebrews 4:14–16). How are you doing with the challenge at the end of the chapter (see the last paragraph)? Have you felt the effects—have you felt God's rest—in your life in any meaningful way since taking the challenge?

CHAPTER SIX

OUR HIGH PRIEST

Hebrews 4:15–5:10

1. Do you find it difficult to live out God's desires for you? What seems to be the most recent challenge in your Christianity?

2. Read Hebrews 4:15–16. When is the best time for you to draw near to Jesus? How often throughout a day would you say that you turn to Him for help? Share some stories of how you have experienced His help lately.

3. In Hebrews 5:1–4, the author of Hebrews illustrates what it means that Jesus is our high priest by explaining what the high priests were like during the time of Moses.

   How do those verses strike you: Do they make you think of individuals in your own life who have those characteristics? Do they cause you to reflect on your own life and how developed your character is in alignment with Christ? Do they help you have any new perspectives about Jesus as your high priest?

4. Read Hebrews 5:5–6. Explain how knowing that Jesus is our high priest touches you at an emotional level? Read Psalms 2 and 110 in their entirety and see if they help you get a fuller picture of the role that Jesus has (or will have) over us. How do we see Jesus'

role dimly in our lives as compared to His role in our eternity, like Paul realized as recorded in 1 Corinthians 13:12?

5. Hebrews 5:7–10 are challenging verses. Take the verses one at a time and see if you can recall the explanation of these phrases from the chapter:

    a. Hebrews 5:7—"from death" or "out of death."

    b. Hebrews 5:8—"He learned obedience."

    c. Hebrews 5:9—"having been made perfect."

    d. Hebrews 5:9—"He became to all those who obey Him the source of eternal salvation."

6. What does this phrase mean in your life now: "Yes, Jesus saved me in the past, but Jesus also saves me now because He is my high priest"?

CHAPTER SEVEN

FROM MILK TO MATURITY

Hebrews 5:11–6:3

1. Rate yourself on a scale of 1 to 10 on how mature you think you are (10 being supermature). Would others agree?

2. Hebrews 5:11 indicates that it is possible for Christians to become dull of hearing (Hebrews 6:12 has the same word and it is translated "sluggish" in the NASB). What are some causes of this "hearing loss"?

    Christians can suffer from *selective hearing loss*: They hear what they want to hear and don't hear what they don't want to hear. Have you seen this in anyone? Does this happen in you? How can we avoid this dysfunction?

3. Hebrews 5:12–13 tells us that we have to be lifelong learners, "accustomed to the word of righteousness." Do you feel like you know the Bible? What have you learned in the last six months about the Bible that you didn't know before? How can we make sure we stay learning?

4. If we are all to be teachers (Hebrews 5:12), how does that square with James 3:1?

5. This chapter talked about three descriptive pairs of what a mature

Christian looks like based on Hebrews 5:14–6:3. Do any of those describe you?

According to Hebrews 6:3, we are pretty capable people; so why do we still need to depend on God? How have you depended on God lately, and how has He revealed to you that you can depend on Him? What do you say to a person who is going through a hard time and doesn't feel like God is there for him or her?

Chapter Eight

GREAT EXPECTATIONS

Hebrews 6:4–9

1. Do you think true, genuine Christians can fall away from the faith? If so, how far away do you think they can fall? Can they totally turn their backs on Jesus?

2. Hebrews 6:4–9 is one of the most controversial passages in the entire Bible. Why do you think that is? And how do you think we should discuss it if we disagree with each other? Can two opposing views of the same passage both be right?

3. Read Hebrews 6:4–6. In the original language (Greek), the sentence begins with "For it is impossible…" Have you ever known anyone who has fallen away from the Lord and it was impossible for you to "renew them again to repentance"? Share your stories.

4. Read Hebrews 6:6 from a couple of different translations and compare the differences. How is it that a Christian who has fallen away *crucifies to themselves the Son of God*? Translations differ on how they word the last clause. The NASB says "and put Him to open shame." Do you remember how it was explained in the chapter? Have you known anyone who at one time trusted in Jesus and now treats Him as worthless, or even vile? How does that impact your heart? What can we do about it?

5. Read Hebrews 6:7–8.

    a. How are you doing with allowing the rain of God's Word and the cultivation by others work the soil of your soul?

    b. To be "cursed" and "burned" does not mean *going to hell*. Read these passages to get an idea of how the word "cursed" is used: Galatians 3:13; James 3:10; 2 Peter 2:14. Then discuss.

    c. Read these passages to get an idea of how the word "burned" is used: Genesis 19:24; Leviticus 10:2; Joshua 7:15; 2 Samuel 22:9; 2 Kings 1:10–14; Daniel 3:22–26; Amos 1:4, 7, 10, 12, 14; 2:2, 5; Luke 9:54; John 15:6; 1 Corinthians 3:13–15; Hebrews 11:34; Jude 23. Then discuss the variety of ways God's Word uses 'fire' and 'burning.' How might this variety of understanding about these words (and their equivalent) help us not jump to the wrong conclusion about the phrase "ends up being burned" in Hebrews 6:8?

6. In Hebrews 6:9, the author encourages the believers. How does that verse strengthen the argument that Christians can fall away from their faith? And how does that verse strengthen us as Christians to stay close to the Lord and not drift away from what we have heard?

CHAPTER NINE

SATISFACTION

Hebrews 6:10–20

1. What is the latest thing that you have pursued that has made you happy? (For example, buying something, doing something, going somewhere.)

2. Read Hebrews 6:10–12. This says we love God by each one of us being involved in ministry to the saints.

   a. Is that the only way we love God (John 14:21, 23)? Is that the primary way we love God? Can we say we love God without doing that?

   b. Hebrews 6:12 cautions us against becoming sluggish. How can we avoid that?

3. Read Hebrews 6:13–15. This is a specific reference to Genesis 22:16–17. Read the context of Genesis 22:16–17. What is that an account of? How did Abraham contribute to his own satisfaction in the Genesis account? How would that apply to us today?

4. Hebrews 6:16–18 mentions that God has given us a promise and He sealed it with an oath. How intense is an "oath" in the Bible

217

according to these passages: Matthew 5:33; 14:6–9; 26:71–72; Luke 1:67–77; Acts 2:30; James 5:12? How seriously do we take the sealing of God's promises with the oath or covenant of the blood of His Son, Jesus? How has that affected you lately?

5. Hebrews 6:11, 18, and 19 all talk about "hope." Do these verses describe your life? Why or why not? Is it possible that, no matter what life brings, we can live a hope-filled life? Explain.

6. Hebrews 6:19–20 indicates that we can enter behind the veil (we can come to the Lord at any time). Read Hebrews 4:15–16; 7:19, 25; 10:1, 22. What do all these verses encourage us to do? Are you doing that regularly? How can we encourage each other in this endeavor?

Chapter Ten

A PICTURE IS WORTH A THOUSAND WORDS

Hebrews 7:1–10

1. An exercise, just for fun: Find photographs, or pictures, and without revealing them to others in the group, use words to describe not only what you see, but what you feel, and what you anticipate will happen in the picture. See how accurately the rest of the group can "experience" the picture as you do.

2. Hebrews 7:1 reflects back to Genesis 14 (which you can read for yourself if you want to—however, read it carefully, as it can be hard to follow). As Melchizedek did with Abraham, do you believe that Jesus meets us where we are and blesses us? How have you experienced the blessing of Jesus in your life lately?

3. Hebrews 7:2 paints a picture of Jesus as our King. Do you think it is hard for people—even Christians—to follow Jesus as their King? Why or why not?

4. Some people think that Melchizedek was actually Jesus appearing in the Old Testament. They think this because of what Hebrews 7:3 says. What do you think? (Make sure you read that verse carefully and give a solid defense.)

5. Abraham honored Melchizedek by giving him a tenth off the top of his choicest spoils (Hebrews 7:4–6). If honor is tangibly shown through giving of a tithe (a tenth), how are you doing with this? Do we make excuses for not showing Jesus honor in this manner? If so, why do you think we do this?

    Second Corinthians 9:7 helps us understand the attitude we ought to have when we give. What attitude do you have around giving? Do you do it freely or under compulsion?

6. Hebrews 7:6–7 alludes to the fact that Jesus is greater than us. Who or what is greater in your life than Jesus?

7. How about that last question (Hebrews 7:8–10): "Is Jesus superior to everyone else in our lives?" How are we doing at standing up for Jesus in the public square, around our friends, at work, in our homes? Do we treat Him with respect as Abraham did with Melchizedek? Why or why not?

CHAPTER ELEVEN

PERFECT PATHWAY

Hebrews 7:11–28

1. There are two kinds of people: Those who are spiritually minded and those who are not. What percentage of people do you think are spiritually minded in America? Why do you think more people are not spiritually minded?

2. No matter if you believe it or not, one person in the group try to convince the rest in the room why there is only one pathway to God. Another person in the group, take the opposite position and likewise try to convince the rest in the room that there are many pathways to God. Now, debate it with each other. Read John 14:6; Acts 4:12; 1 Timothy 2:3–6; and Hebrews 7:11–19, and continue to discuss how many pathways there are that lead to God.

3. Hebrews 7:14 indicates that Jesus is from the tribe of Judah, not Levi. Read the blessing that Jacob gave to Judah and his descendants to see how it describes who Jesus is (Genesis 49:8–10).

4. In this chapter we read a Holocaust story from the book *The Seamstress*, by Sara Tuvel Bernstein. Is what you read your image of the Lord? How does your image differ? How does your life reflect those truths?

5. Read Hebrews 7:20–25. Do you draw near to God through Jesus? How does that look for you? How is it that Jesus helps you?

   This chapter clarifies the fact that Jesus "save[s] forever" (verse 25). It is a reference to Jesus saving us from the power of sin in our lives—those things that get in the way of our drawing near to God. How have you witnessed Jesus saving you or someone else from the power of sin?

6. Remember my story about being scared at the toboggan chute and how people are afraid to totally trust Jesus? Do you know someone who struggles to trust Jesus completely? What do you think gets in the way? Read Hebrews 7:26–28. Does that help you place your total trust in Jesus? What holds you back (or someone you know) from completely surrendering yourself to Him?

CHAPTER TWELVE

WHAT'S UP IN HEAVEN?

Hebrews 8:1–6

1. When you think about Jesus as your high priest, what images or thoughts come into your head about Him?

2. Read Hebrews 8:1. There is a lot of truth packed into that one verse. What strikes you most about that verse?

    Read the following passages that translate the plural "heavens" as a singular "heaven" (all of which are plural in the original language): Matthew 5:12, 16; 16:19; Luke 10:20; Ephesians 3:15; Philippians 3:20; Colossians 1:20 (in 1:16 it's the same Greek word, same form, but translated in the plural). In Hebrews the plural is translated both ways: Hebrews 9:23; 12:23 (along with this passage here, 8:1). So, what do you make of all of this? Why do you think the plural is translated into the singular?

3. Hebrews 8:2 indicates there is a place of worship in heaven. What kind of a reaction do you have to that truth? Do you believe these things? Why or why not?

4. Read Hebrews 8:3–5. The quote at the end of verse 5 is from Exodus 25:40. Read Exodus 24 and 25 to see the context and the account behind that quote. Do you think Moses saw the

true tabernacle in order to have the pattern to make the earthly one?

Places of worship are shadows of the true tabernacle. Do you think churches ought to build beautiful sanctuaries because they are to be copies or shadows of the true place of worship that we will have for eternity? Or do you think they should just be functional, basic, and we shouldn't spend money on the places where we gather to worship? Why?

5. Hebrews 8:6 says that Jesus is our mediator. He died for us on the cross (many of us understand that part of His mediation), yet He mediates for us all the time. Read John 17 in its entirety to see how Jesus mediated for us when He was here, and discuss how Jesus mediates for us now and whether it is anything like He did then.

6. Do you believe our Christian experience both now and forever is on the shoulders of Jesus? And our role in the relationship is to walk by faith in Him? Read Matthew 11:28–30; 2 Corinthians 4:16–18; 5:6–8; 1 John 1:6–7 (maybe you can think of more passages that speak about our walk of faith), and discuss how Jesus bears our burdens.

Chapter Thirteen

WE CAN'T—WE WILL—BUT UNTIL

Hebrews 8:6–13

1. Read Hebrews 8:6–7. These Jewish Christians had a hard time setting aside the old covenant that God made with Israel (the law). It became habit for them. What are some common "bad habits" or ways we live that we have picked up from our upbringings?

   The number one bad habit of Christians when we want to partner with Christ is: *work harder, add more restrictions, be more diligent to obey the law (even legalism)*. Do you know of anyone who promotes this? Do you promote this?

2. Hebrews 8:8–12 contains the longest Old Testament quote found in the New Testament. It comes from Jeremiah 31:31–34. Who are the people this new covenant is addressed to (see Hebrews 8:8, 10)?

   a. Read Romans 11:7, 13–27 (it is a challenging passage, so take it slow and think through what you are reading). What does this Romans passage tell us as Gentiles (non-Jewish people) about being a part of God's eternal plans He made with Israel?

   b. In Hebrews 8:9, the New American Standard Bible says God "did not care for them." The same word (in the Greek) for that phrase is found in Hebrews 2:3, where we may "neglect" so great a salvation. It's also found in Matthew 22:5; 1 Timothy 1:14; and 2 Peter 1:12. Read those passages and get a feel for what it means. According to the context of Hebrews 8:9, why did God neglect the Israelites? Why would God neglect us today (Romans 1:20–32, especially verse 24)?

3. Remember the story of climbing the mountain with Brent and finding a large valley that was a metaphor for the valley we are in today called grace (Hebrews 8:13, somewhere between the old or first covenant and the new covenant)? How are you doing in drawing near to the Lord? How are you doing living in this age of grace? What are some things that get in the way of drawing near to the Lord?

CHAPTER FOURTEEN

THE HEIGHT OF HOLINESS

Hebrews 9:1–14

1. When you think about God, what are some words or phrases that come to your mind?

2. Hebrews 9:1–5 describes the tabernacle. Have you ever heard about "Aaron's rod which budded"? Three men named Korah, Dathan, and Abiram revolted. They thought they should be the leaders of Israel, above Aaron (the brother of Moses). Because of their rebellion, 14,700 people died. Now read Numbers 17:1–18:5 for *the rest of the story*.

    Do we have that holy reverence or holy fear of God today? Should we? Why or why not?

3. Hebrews 9:6–7 is a very condensed version of what happens on the Day of Atonement (Leviticus 16–17). On that day the function of the high priest revealed that the way to God was really blocked; Hebrews 9:8–10 tells us why.

    How have you seen people try, in this day and age, to make their consciences perfect in ways that do not align with biblical Christianity? How might we talk to them about how rites, rituals, even religion will never get us over the hurdle of our hearts?

4. There seems to be a dramatic hinge or shift in the text in Hebrews 9:11–12. What is it?

5. What does "redemption" mean (Hebrews 9:12)? How has the redemption that Jesus brought to you changed your life? Does Hebrews 9:13–14 describe any of that change?

6. There is a very clear contrast in Hebrews 9:14 between dead works and serving the living God. Discuss how this contrast shows up in real life. Where is your heart: Is it focused on dead works or on serving the living God? How are you serving Him?

CHAPTER FIFTEEN

THE THREEFOLD ROLE OF JESUS

Hebrews 9:15–28

1. If you had to identify the primary role that you play in life, what would it be (mom, dad, husband, wife, teacher, lawyer, doctor, etc.)? Is that the role that ought to be primary in your life?

2. Hebrews 9:15 begins by telling us that Jesus is the mediator of a new covenant. Do you remember the illustration of a last will and testament? Do you have a will? If you do, do you believe it will be carried out after you die? If you answered yes, you are acting in faith. Because of the death of Jesus we can relate to God in faith. How do you relate to God by faith?

3. In the middle of Hebrews 9:15 it says that Jesus died to redeem us from our transgressions (how we step over the line and sin against God). Do you know anyone who is "near-comatose to the reality" that they are far from God? Is there any way that you can be a "St. Bernard" to them to rouse them from their slumber?

4. Read Hebrews 9:22. The two exceptions under the law that didn't need cleansing by blood are found in Leviticus 5:11–13 and Numbers 31:22–23. Now read Hebrews 9:23–24. Have you ever thought that Jesus appears before God "for us"? What

intellectual and/or emotional reaction do you have when you read that truth?

5. Read Hebrews 9:25–26. Remember Jeremy's explanation of "at the consummation of the ages"? How has Jesus liberated you from the power of sin in your life lately?

6. Jesus is the evaluator. He will be the judge (cf. John 5:22, 27). Hebrews 9:27 seems to indicate this. Did you realize that there are at least three judgments in the Bible? They include the judgment of Christians (1 Corinthians 3:10–15; 2 Corinthians 5:10), the judgment at the end of the tribulation for those who went through it (Matthew 25:31–46), and the great white throne judgment at the end of the millennial kingdom (Revelation 20:11–15). How much do you think about standing before the Lord Jesus and being judged by Him?

7. Hebrews 9:28 says we must eagerly await Jesus. How are you eagerly awaiting Him?

Chapter Sixteen

LIFTING THE BARRIER AND BURDEN OF SIN

Hebrews 10:1–25

1. Hebrews 10:1–4 indicates that we can't lift the burden of sin by what we do. Have you ever heard someone say, in some form or fashion, "God will accept me because I'm a good person"? What is wrong with that logic, if anything? How would you go about telling that person that his or her logic is wrong? (Maybe role-play this scenario with others in your group to practice.)

2. Hebrews 10:5–10 says that through Jesus and what He has done, we, as Christians, have been sanctified. Remember the illustration of the movie *The Princess Diaries* that explained that there are two kinds of sanctification? The technical or theological terms for those two types are "positional sanctification" and "progressive sanctification." Given what was said in the chapter, can you explain the difference?

Hebrews 10:8–9 (quoting Psalm 40:6–8) reveals the contrast between the law and Jesus for making us sanctified. Read Psalm 51:16–17; Isaiah 1:10–17; and Isaiah 66:3–4, and see what matters more to God than bringing sacrifices to the tabernacle or temple.

3. Hebrews 10:13 tells us that enemies are being placed under the feet of Jesus. According to Psalm 2; Romans 1:20–32; Galatians 5:16–26; Hebrews 2:14 (Ephesians 6:10–20), what are some of the enemies that wage war against us and the things of the Lord? Are you in any battles now? Do you feel like you are winning lately or not? How can we fight together—bear each other's burdens (Galatians 6:2)? How can we avoid battle fatigue?

4. Read Hebrews 10:19–25. Follow the three times in this section that the author writes "let us." How are we doing on these?

    a. Are we drawing near to the Lord? Why or why not?

    b. Are we clinging to the truth? Why or why not? Do you think people in our culture are slipping away from the absolute truth of God and are believing more and more of the lies that are out there? What can we do to help stop the sliding away from God and His truth?

    c. Are we encouraging each other? Why or why not? What have you done in the past two weeks to encourage someone else, or to spur someone on to love and good deeds? How have you been encouraged by someone else in the family of God in the last two weeks? (How you answer this may help you see if you are living out Hebrews 10:24–25.)

CHAPTER SEVENTEEN

IT IS RIGHT

Hebrews 10:26–39

1. Sometimes knowing what is right is not easy. Is it right that the end justifies the means? Is it okay to holler at people because they "deserve it"? Is it okay to lie in some circumstances? Is it right to turn a blind eye to somebody else's sin as long as it's not hurting someone else?

2. Read Hebrews 10:26–27. The chapter explained what it means that there no longer remains a sacrifice for sins for Christians who willfully go on sinning. How do we *bring our sacrifices over and over again to God*, as if to justify or make amends for our misbehavior?

   Hebrews 10:27 sounds pretty intense. How often do you think about your potential to make God very angry (Psalm 79:5; Isaiah 26:11; Zephaniah 1:18; 3:8; Zechariah 8:2; and 2 Thessalonians 1:7)? What does it mean to have a healthy fear of God? How does that fear show up in your life, and how do you know that it is a healthy fear (versus unhealthy)?

3. Hebrews 10:28–31 continues the warning that the Lord will judge us.

233

a. Hebrews 10:28 is true; just read Numbers 35:30 or Deuteronomy 17:2–6.

b. How does the Lord carry out His vengeance according to Deuteronomy 32:35–36 and Psalms 50:1–6 and 135:14? What seems to accompany His vengeance? How do you view God's vengeance? Do these passages change your view at all?

4. Hebrews 10:32–34 indicates that we are to keep our focus on eternity even if it means we forfeit some of our creature comforts (Matthew 6:19–21). How willing do you think we are in America to give up our creature comforts for the Lord (if He brings us into a difficult time)? How willing do you think you are?

5. Hebrews 10:35–39 tells us not to shrink back and instead to live by faith. What can we do to spur each other on (Hebrews 10:24–25; see also 3:12–13)? How have you encouraged other Christians lately to press on? Is there anyone who has shrunk back that you need to talk to?

Have you had any hardships lately that God is calling you to endure? Are you a part of a church family who is helping you to bear your burdens (Galatians 6:2)?

Chapter Eighteen

A FAITH THAT IS FIT

Hebrews 11:1–40

1. If you had to assess how healthy your faith is, how would you rank it on a scale of 1 to 10 (1 being weak, lame, feeble, and 10 being solid, strong, healthy, fit)?

2. Hebrews 11:1 gives a definition of *faith*. Some scholars say it isn't a complete definition. Do you think its definition of *faith* is complete? Why do you think some say it isn't complete? What do you think they see that might be missing from the definition?

   Hope can slip through our fingers and fade away. Have you had anything in your life that you have hoped for and it seems like hope is being dashed to pieces?

3. Hebrews 11:6 is a key passage for the whole eleventh chapter of Hebrews. Read it carefully together. Remember what the chapter said about the two words: "comes" and "seek"? They are present participles (a continuous action in the present). How would you say you are doing on "coming" to the Lord and "seeking" Him today? What gets in the way of this?

4. On a scale of one to ten (one being very little and ten being a lot), how much have you thought about the fact that God is a rewarder of those who seek Him? Explain why you chose that number.

a. Hebrews 11:7–22 highlights how God will reward us in the future. Verses 10, 14 and 16 are key verses. In what ways do you live today in light of eternity?

b. Hebrews 11:23–35a reveals that a life lived by faith may result in seeing the reward of God even in this life. Have you experienced God's reward (seeing Him miraculously working or doing amazing things) even now in your life as you walk by faith? How so?

c. Yet Hebrews 11:35b–38 paints a different picture. Have you seen Christians who seem to go through difficult times and God does not seem to rescue them out of it?

What do you think of this statement: "There's no good way to answer the deep problem of pain without a deep hope and faith in God and His eternity"?

5. Hebrews 11:39–40 states that it is through faith that we gain approval before God—approval for responsibility in the future. The only way to please God is by faith (Hebrews 11:6). How fit is your faith? And how can we encourage each other today in our faith (Hebrews 3:12–13; 10:23–25)?

CHAPTER NINETEEN

RUN WITH ENDURANCE

Hebrews 12:1–17

1. According to Hebrews 12:1, God sets a course before us to run. Ephesians 2:10 seems to support that as well. Have you ever veered off the course that God desires for you to run? How can we know if we are on the course or off the course? *(Hint: the rest of the passage will help us with this.)*

2. Hebrews 12:1 tells us to lay aside encumbrances and sin. We can identify "sin" relatively easily (we can argue what is sin and what isn't, but for the most part we know what sin is), but what are some "encumbrances" in your life that get in the way of you running well?

3. Hebrews 12:2 tells us where to keep our focus. When we help others through their struggles, we must remember they need Jesus more than anything else. Jesus is not very tangible, so how do we explain to others that they need Jesus? How can we help them find Him?

4. Hebrews 12:5–6 indicates that we ought to expect discipline from the Lord and that He disciplines us because He loves us. How have you experienced the discipline of the Lord lately? (Remember, "discipline" means "child training; guidance to develop responsible living before the Lord.")

237

Part of God's discipline is "scourges." Read all the other times this same word is used and see if you can determine what it means: Matthew 10:17; 20:19; 23:34; Mark 10:34; Luke 18:33; John 19:1. Has God ever brought scourging in your life?

5. This chapter lays out what the author of Hebrews meant when he wrote that God's discipline brings "life" (Hebrews 12:9–14). Can you identify those four things in verses 10–14? How have these things been seen in your life?

6. Finally, we are in this together (Hebrews 12:15–17). Have you helped others not to fall short of the grace of God?

CHAPTER TWENTY

ARE WE LISTENING?

Hebrews 12:18–29

1. Hebrews presents five warnings to Christians. Review the warning passages:

    1. Don't drift! The danger of neglecting our salvation (2:1–4).

    2. Don't develop a hard heart and miss the kingdom rest (3:1–4:16).

    3. Beware of permanent dullness (5:11–6:20).

    4. Don't continue in willful sin (10:19–29).

    5. Don't fail to heed God's speaking (12:25–29).

    6. Which of these have you struggled with lately?

2. God speaks to us today. How do you know when you are listening to Him (see the first sentence of Hebrews 12:25)?

3. Do you remember the ways that God speaks to us? How balanced are you at allowing these three ways to be used by God to speak to you? Do you think there needs to be a balance?

    a. The Bible: 2 Timothy 3:10–11; 2 Peter 1:20–21.

b. Prayer: Romans 10:13; Philippians 4:6–7; James 1:5.

c. Other people: Hebrews 3:12–13; 10:24–25; Ephesians 5:19; Colossians 3:16.

4. On a scale of 1 to 10 (10 being the best), rate how well you listen. Are you a good listener? Review the obstacles to listening. Did any of those hit home? Talk through the obstacles that you face to being a good listener to God, and discuss how we might help each other overcome those obstacles.

5. Review the three reasons in the chapter why we need to listen to our Lord (Hebrews 12:25–29).

a. Second Chronicles 16:9 is a great verse to meditate on. How do you picture God's watchful eye? Does that verse capture it for you, or do you have a different view?

b. How can we spur each other on to keep our attention on eternal things more so than temporal or temporary things?

c. Do you agree or disagree with this statement: *This life is a training time to get us ready to serve the Lord in eternity, so let's live this day in light of that day.* Are you listening?

CHAPTER TWENTY-ONE

ACCEPTABLE SERVICE

Hebrews 13:1–14

1. Read Hebrews 13:1–3. On a scale of 1 to 10 (1 is poor; 10 is great), if you had to rate yourself on how well you love other Christians, what number would you give yourself and why?

    We don't really experience persecution like they did back in the Roman Empire when Christianity was just starting, do we? Have you witnessed anyone being mistreated for his or her faith? Have you ever been mistreated because you are a Christian? How can we show love to other Christians who are persecuted (either locally or abroad)?

2. Hebrews 13:4 is very clear. Do you think our society is beyond hope when it comes to honoring marriage and keeping the marriage bed pure? What can we do to uphold God's standards on this issue? Christians get divorced as often as non-Christians; Christians defile the marriage bed (they fool around). Do you agree or disagree with the following statement? Let's face it; our sexuality wages war against this verse. What can we do to honor God in this area?

3. Hebrews 13:5–6 emphasizes trusting the Lord. Have you ever been betrayed by someone? How did you handle it? Even if

everybody in the whole world turned their backs on you, or you lost every earthly possession, could you say with confidence these verses?

4. Read Hebrews 13:7. Have you ever taught someone else spiritual truths (as Matthew 28:19–20 tells us we ought to be doing)? How can we expect people to be able to watch our conduct when we have failed in many ways? How can we balance 1 Corinthians 11:1 with 1 Timothy 1:15?

5. Remember the workout in the chapter regarding being strengthened by grace (Hebrews 13:8–9)? Which one of the three exercises do you need to work on most?

6. Does your focus align with the message of Hebrews 13:14? Why or why not?

Chapter Twenty-Two

A COMMUNITY COMMITTED TO BEING CHRIST'S COMPANIONS

Hebrews 13:15–25

1. The chapter began by stating that the foundational element of a healthy church is to set the right tone. Do you agree or disagree? Why?

2. Review the three areas where we can work on setting the right tone: praising God, loving one another, and following our leaders (Hebrews 13:15–17).

   a. Each one of those areas has its challenges in order to do it well. Which one do you think is the most difficult to do, and why?

   b. Looking around, can you identify people in the room who are good at helping to create the right tone at your church? What characteristics and behaviors do you see in them that help with that positive feeling of being Christ's companions?

3. Hebrews 13:18–21 is all about prayer. How is your prayer life? How can we know that we have a good prayer life?

   a. Do we have a good prayer life just because we pray often, or does it have to do with the content of our prayers (what we are praying for)?

b. Read Hebrews 13:18. What was the request to pray for in that verse? Now read Hebrews 13:20–21. What was the prayer for in that verse?

Does that describe the content of what we pray for when we are praying for others? If we are going to be a community committed to being Christ's companions, should it be?

4. Three things are mentioned in the chapter that we must be committed to if we are going to grow. How are you doing on them (letting the Word penetrate, accountability to motivate, and grace to permeate)?

What are some things that can kill grace (going against Hebrews 13:25)? How can we avoid them or do away with them?

BIBLIOGRAPHY

Aland, Kurt, Matthew Black, Carlo M. Martini, Bruce M. Metzger, and Allen Wikgren, eds. *The Greek New Testament*. 3rd ed. Stuttgart, Germany: United Bible Societies, 1983.

Associated Press. "All 33 Chilean Miners Rescued in Flawless Operation." Fox News, October 13, 2010, accessed January 20, 2014. www.foxnews.com/world/2010/10/12/rescued-chilean-miner-returns-surface.

Atkinson, David J., David F. Field, Arthur Holmes, and Oliver O'Donovan, eds. *New Dictionary of Christian Ethics and Pastoral Theology*. Downers Grove, IL: InterVarsity, 1995.

Beale, G. K., and D. A. Carson, eds. *Commentary on the New Testament Use of the Old Testament*. Grand Rapids, MI: Baker Academic, 2007.

Bernstein, Sara Tuvel, Louise Loots Thornton, and Marlene Bernstein Samuels. *The Seamstress: A Memoir of Survival*. New York: Berkley Books, 1997.

BILD International. "Essentials of Sound Doctrine" course, material on I Clement and the Didache, as well as Gnostic heresy. Ames, Iowa.

De Haan, M. R. *Hebrews: Twenty-Six Simple Studies in God's Plan for Victorious Living*. Grand Rapids, MI: Lamplighter Books, 1959.

Douglas, Lloyd C. *The Robe*. New York: Houghton Mifflin Company, 1942.

Durant, Will. *The Story of Civilization*, vol. 3. New York: Simon & Schuster, 1944.

Evans, Morris, Melvin Grove Kyle, Edgar Mullins, John Nuelsen, and James Orr, eds. *International Standard Bible Encyclopedia*, 4 volumes. Grand Rapids, MI: Eerdmans, 1995.

Friberg, Timothy, Barbara Friberg, Neva F. Miller. *Analytical Lexicon of the Greek New Testament*. Grand Rapids, MI: Baker Books, 2000.

Gingrich, F. Wilbur, and Frederick W. Danker, *A Greek-English Lexicon of the New Testament and Other Early Christian Literature*. 2nd ed. Chicago: University of Chicago Press, 1983.

Handwerk, Brian. "Yellowstone Has Bulged as Magma Pocket Swells." National Geographic News, January 19, 2011, accessed January 19, 2014. http://news.nationalgeographic.com/news/2011/01/110119-yellowstone-park-supervolcano-eruption-magma-science.

Ironside, H. A. *Hebrews: An Ironside Expository Commentary* Grand Rapids, MI: Kregel, 2008.

Lane, William L. *Word Biblical Commentary: Hebrews 1–8*. Dallas: Word, Incorporated, 2002.

Lang, G. H. *The Epistle to the Hebrews*. 2nd ed. Miami Springs, FL: Conley & Schoettle, 1985.

Lenehan, Arthur F. ed. *The Best of Bits and Pieces*. Fairfield: NJ: Economic Press, 1994.

Lewis, C. S. *The Problem of Pain*. New York: MacMillan, 1962.

McNab, Chris, ed. *The Roman Army: The Greatest War Machine of the Ancient World*. Oxford: Osprey, 2010.

Oberholtzer, Thomas Kem. "The Kingdom Rest in Hebrews 3:1–4:13." *Bibliotheca Sacra*, April–June 1988.

O'Brien, Peter T. *The Letter to the Hebrews*. The Pillar New Testament Commentary. Grand Rapids, MI: Eerdmans, 2010.

"A Picture Is Worth a Thousand Words." Phrase Finder, accessed January 20, 2014. www.phrases.org.uk/meanings/a-picture-is-worth-a-thousand-words.html.

"Arrogance," Sermon Illustrations, accessed January 19, 2014. www.sermonillustrations.com/a-z/a/arrogance.htm.

Shaara, Jeff. *Gods and Generals*. New York: Ballantine, 1996.

Swindoll, Charles R., *The Tale of the Tardy Oxcart: And 1,501 Other Stories*. Nashville, TN: Word Publishing, 1998.

Thompson, Todd, "Still Waters." *A Slice of Life to Go*, December 18, 2008, accessed January 18, 2014. www.asliceoflifetogo.com/2008/12/18/still-waters.

Thompson, Todd, "Meltdown." *A Slice of Life to Go*, March 21, 2006, accessed January 29, 2014. www.asliceoflifetogo.com/2006/3/21/meltdown.

Wachter, Dana, and Lisa Stark. "Tired? Study Says Americans Need More Sleep." ABC News, February 28, 2008, accessed January 20, 2014. http://abcnews.go.com/Health/OnCall/story?id=4361378&page=1.

Wakefield, Norm. *Perceptive Listening: Building Stronger Relationships*. Class notes, "Building Biblical Relationships," Phoenix Seminary.

Walvoord, John F., and Roy B. Zuck, eds. *The Bible Knowledge Commentary: An Exposition of the Scriptures*. Wheaton, IL: Victor Books, 1983.

Wilkin, Robert N. *Confident in Christ*. Irving, TX: Grace Evangelical Society, 1999.